Financial Freedom *for*
Special
Needs
Families

FINANCIAL FREEDOM *for* SPECIAL NEEDS FAMILIES

9 Building Blocks to Reduce Stress, Preserve Benefits, and Create a Fulfilling Future

ROB WRUBEL, CFP®

Published by Rosalibean Publishing LLC

Copyright © 2017 by Rob Wrubel

First printing 2017

Printed in the United States of America

20 19 18 17 16 1 2 3 4 5

ISBN 978-0-9966592-1-5

Library of Congress Control Number: 2017957452

To Benjie, Sarah, Annie and Kelly

Contents

Introduction

In 2001, I started a second career as a financial planner. This was a few months after my first child was born, and it was a hectic, exciting, and joyful time. There was so much for me to learn both as a new father and as a new financial planner. During the day, I studied about investment ideas, tax opportunities and regulations, retirement plans, and financial planning ideas; and I prepared for the series of securities licenses I'd need in order to invest my clients' savings. At night I bounced my son on my knee, sang songs, walked around the neighborhood, and urged him to sleep through the night. It was incredibly exciting to watch this newborn change every single day.

As a financial planner, I soon started to work on my own family's financial plan. Like so many people, I did not have a will in place, I wanted to save more for retirement, and I needed life insurance. I started thinking about preschool, camps, and colleges—and how to pay for it all. With all I was learning in my career, I quickly came to understand what needed to be in place for my own family.

Soon I was working with other families on typical planning. I became proficient in helping them use investment tools—IRAs, 529 college savings plans, term life insurance, stocks, bonds, and mutual funds—and I was starting to understand how to help bring all of these together to help people feel like they could retire comfortably, happily pay for college, and invest wisely. I was learning that much of financial planning comes down to encouraging people to save, pay off debt, and invest for the future, and I found that my clients started to feel better after making even small changes. The technical work was important for my clients, but the coaching, support, and partnerships we created were what made them feel confident and optimistic about their financial outlook.

My second child, a daughter, was born eighteen months after my son. In the delivery room, it was clear something was different about her. As I first looked at her, I remarked that her nose appeared unusual and that she was small.

Within seconds the nurses whisked her away. That really got my attention. Something wasn't just different; something had them worried. They took my newborn daughter straight to the neonatal intensive care unit. The next few hours were a blur, and I don't remember much other than walking around the hospital halls in a daze and signing a consent-to-treat form somewhere along the way.

That evening, our doctor came into the room. She had a somber look, and it was clear she had something to tell us—our Sarah was a sick girl and she had Down syndrome. She also let us know that Sarah would need blood transfusions and that a few specialists were going to take a look at her—starting with an oncologist and a cardiologist, followed by a series of other "ologists."

Our pediatrician was the first to talk to us about having a baby with Down syndrome. She was compassionate and told us we would have to let go of the life we thought we would have, which would take time, but in doing so we would be better able to embrace the life we were about to live. Needless to say, we were a wreck and were doing all we could just to hold it together emotionally.

Health complications kept my daughter in the hospital for the next six weeks. She eventually had heart surgery when she was six months old. Those were long, difficult times. One of the cardiologists was experienced with newborns with Down syndrome and kept telling us that Sarah would surprise us throughout her recovery and all she would bring to the family.

We were introduced to a new set of specialists. My daughter had speech, occupational, and physical therapy.

After she left the hospital, I realized the doctors were right: our life would be different in so many ways, including in our financial and legal planning.

Back then, the internet was in its early stages, and so useful information about families like mine was not readily available. I spent time meeting with lawyers and accountants. I met with the heads of disabilities agencies trying to figure out what would happen next. I attended a meeting of the local Down syndrome association in the hospital a few doors down from where my daughter lived in the NICU.

I even tried talking with people at the Social Security Administration to understand the benefits programs. It did not go well when I was told, "If we made it easy, everyone would want the benefits."

In a short time, I had discovered appropriate planning techniques to use for my family and was now ready to help others. I realized that providing this specialized type of financial planning would allow me to make a real difference for my clients.

These events changed my life—as a father, community member,

and financial planner. My family has a great time together, and Sarah leads us in laughter and song. I've come to understand how our differences make us stronger and how each member of our community has something to offer. My research and understanding have led me to become an expert in financial and legal planning for families like ours, and I've met the most incredible people because of my daughter and what we've been through.

By the time my third child, another daughter, was born, I began to understand that effective financial planning meant listening to others' concerns and fears and that there was much more to my career than technical knowledge.

Here's what I now know: Families often come to my office in a state of fear and anxiety. They are overwhelmed with the decisions they need to make about their financial life and future planning. They are asking themselves countless questions but don't know how to begin to answer them. They want financial freedom and the knowledge that the decisions they make today will provide a comfortable retirement for them, a secure future for their children, and funding to help their family members with disabilities live high-quality, fulfilling, and enjoyable lives.

FINANCIAL FREEDOM

Families who have children with special needs have many distinct stressors, from managing health issues, to navigating school programs, to maintaining benefits, to creating social lives, to interpreting language, to worrying about safety and other concerns. We also have to plan differently for our families. Many of the families I speak with express anxiety at the mention of talking with a lawyer. The thought of looking at finances adds to their worries. The future feels uncertain, painful, and unclear.

This book will help you reduce the stress that comes from having too much debt, no plan for the future, uncertainty about public benefits, and too few funds.

Imagine a day when you wake up and do not feel stressed by your financial burdens. That day can come soon, because you have the ability to change your feelings about your financial status from fear to freedom. You can think about the joys of life—a life in which you fully live each day. By reading this book and following through on the exercises found in it, you will gain freedom by taking control of your planning and not being shackled by worry, debt, or fear.

Families who have children with special needs have unique planning considerations. We have family members who will need our support while we live and will still need support after we pass away. We need to build the best financial lives possible for ourselves. We have to get the right legal plans in place. We need to understand available government benefits (such as Supplemental Security Income and Medicaid-funded services) and the organizations that can support our family members in the future.

This book will help you move from anxiety to aspiration, from confusion to clarity, and from fear to freedom. Many families are uncertain as to how to get their minds around the planning they need to do. Start with a trust? Fund retirement? Pay off student loans? Get life insurance? Reduce credit card debt? There are many options, and each demands time and money. *Financial Freedom for Special Needs Families—9 Building Blocks to Reduce Stress, Preserve Benefits, and Create a Fulfilling Future* provides a structure that will help you tackle your financial and legal planning issues. It also gives you worksheets that will help you make sound decisions for your family.

THE BUILDING BLOCKS

This book uses the metaphor of building a house. No one just starts building a house. Much thought, planning, and design goes into a house before any construction starts. There are many decisions made in the planning stage. Will the house have one floor or two? Will it be in town or in the country? And will it be modern or historic? These are just a few examples. Paint color, room size, furnishings, tile or wood floors, and hundreds of other decisions follow.

The metaphor makes sense to most people as planning for your future is a complex and time-consuming task. Financial considerations such as saving for retirement, funding a trust, getting out of debt, building an emergency fund, and having funds to pay for an exciting and fulfilling life require patience, planning, and commitment. There are many steps to the process, steps which must often be taken at the same time.

Financial freedom does not happen overnight. Like the construction of a house, it often seems there is a lot of activity for a long time with little result. Then, all of a sudden, there is shape, color, and something incredible. In financial terms, that something incredible looks like money in the bank, investments in retirement accounts, a plan to fund a trust, and being debt free. It can take months to years to feel any progress, but then the moment comes when it all starts fitting together and you and your family start to feel optimistic and secure.

The book gives you a series of steps that will help you move forward quickly.

These steps are call Building Blocks, and *Financial Freedom for Special Needs Families—9 Building Blocks to Reduce Stress, Preserve Benefits, and Create a Fulfilling Future* is presented in a specific order. It starts with the dream—What is it you want out of life?—and ends with funding a trust. Each chapter takes you through one of the nine building blocks:

1. Dreaming about Your Future
2. Starting to Design

3. Taking Stock
4. Building a Foundation—The Special-Needs Trust
5. Eliminating Debt Forever
6. Financial Stability
7. Protect Your Family
8. Investing for Your Future
9. Funding the Trust

Each Building Block includes worksheets to help you with brainstorming and making decisions. The first four Building Blocks can be finished in a matter of weeks. These are the planning decisions and the foundational elements you need to move toward financial freedom. The other five Building Blocks take longer to accomplish, but you will see progress as you pay off debts, build emergency funds, and as the money in your retirement and investment accounts begins to grow.

You should complete the worksheets for each chapter before leaping into action. In fact, you probably already have some parts of each Building Block complete, but you may have made a few errors or you don't have a coherent strategy.

As a whole, the Building Blocks will enable you to live free from the worry that you have not done anything to protect yourself and your family member with special needs. You will feel newfound freedom from stress in your financial life. And once you feel this freedom, you can you can turn your thoughts and desires to living the most fulfilling life possible. You will be able to put your energy into enjoying each day, looking forward to the future, and feeling confident that life for your family member with an intellectual or developmental disability will be rewarding, fulfilling, and joyful.

A WORD ON LANGUAGE

This book and the other parts of the Blueprints series strive to use person-centered language. There is no "Down syndrome person." There are only people with Down syndrome. My daughter, your family members, and all the wonderful people with disabilities we meet are people first and are not defined by their labels. There are many times where I used the words "Special-Needs Families" and "Special-Needs Trusts." Part of this is so that you are familiar with the language your attorney, CPA, and financial planner use. The other part has to do with my desire for a language economy that makes this book easier to read. There are many times where sentences would be too long or too confusing if I used "a family with a member who has an intellectual or developmental disability" instead of "special-needs person." When I talk about a specific person, I use people-centered language. When referring to families, trusts, or planning, I use the term "special-needs."

Building Block 1

Dreaming About the Future

"The future belongs to those who believe in the beauty of their dreams."
—**Eleanor Roosevelt**

"Life can only be understood backwards but must be lived forward."
—**Soren Kierkegaard**

You have a crystal ball, a real one that shows the future, sitting in front of you.

What do you see?

What do you *want* to see?

Blueprints for Special-Needs Families is a simple, powerful, and exciting process designed to help you change your financial life and to help you and your family member with special needs live the most fulfilling, enjoyable, and meaningful life possible. It is designed to

1

help you eliminate financial stress and provide for your family in a way you never thought imaginable. Blueprints helps you take control of your future and build the ideal life for your entire family—and the best life possible for your family member with special needs.

We use the model of building a house—a complex event made up of decision after decision after decision. A house needs a vision, a set of plans, a foundation, and a structure. Keep this concept in mind as you begin to build the life of your dreams for you and your family.

Several big decisions must be made before hiring an architect or builder. Before you begin, you need to think about whether you want a ranch house, a split-level house, or a two-story home. Will you need a two-car or three-car garage? Is this house in town or on acreage in the country? Will you need two, three, or four bedrooms? These are basic decisions that must be made based on your family's needs, and you need to have them in mind before you sit down with an architect. The architect will ask you series of questions designed to help you imagine the home you desire and think through the key decisions. At this point, you have not started any building—and you won't until you have a much clearer idea of your needs and goals. You will not start building until you have a plan.

The Blueprints process starts at this moment of planning—before you hire an accountant, lawyer, financial planner, or any other professional. You start with the creative process, which includes your thoughts, dreams, and taking the time to sketch out a vision of the future you wish to see, live, and enjoy. The "beauty of your dreams" can be lived by taking the time to imagine the life you wish to have and working to make it come true.

There are no limits, rules, or guidelines for you to follow as you start down the Blueprints process.

Think about the great inventors and creative people of our time—Thomas Edison, Pablo Picasso, Steve Jobs, Jackson Pollock, J. K.

Rowling. The efforts of these people and thousands like them led to a world where we have light in our homes, computers in our hands, and new ways to look at and perceive the world. These visionaries did not accept the world as it was. If they had, we would be reading books by candlelight and communicating with each other with handwritten, hand-delivered letters.

These inventors and dreamers had a thought before ever designing a project. In a similar way, Blueprints lets you release and use your creative energy as you start down the road to building a life of financial security and peace of mind for your family.

Envisioning the Future

All day long, we walk around with thousands of thoughts streaming through our minds—thoughts about the future and thoughts about the past. They include the thoughts "I am hungry," "I am tired," "I am thrilled," and many more. They take the form of wishes for ourselves and our family member with special needs, and they take the form of concerns, worries, and fears.

Our daily thoughts are disrupted by streaming messages, radio ads, billboards, gossip, directives at work, and questions from family members, but the important thoughts are still there, floating around, disrupted and distracted by the rest of daily life.

We rarely take the time to organize our dreams and desires for the future into a coherent set of messages and goals and to focus our thinking on the positive outcomes and joyful life we should live and wish to live. Too often we are told, "Don't ask for too much" or "You cannot have that." We are told we do not deserve or will never have the life of our dreams. This section of the book is designed to help you focus your emotions and thoughts on the positive outcomes you want for yourself and each member of your family. It will help you put negative impulses aside as you sketch out the happiest, most fulfilling, exciting, and desirable life and goals you want.

You cannot begin building your dream home or drawing up Blueprints without taking the time to write down your dreams and visions. It simply doesn't work.

We find in working with people that the big thoughts of a happy, fulfilling life are there inside but are covered up by negative thinking, prior disappointments, and fear. Yet most of us crave the chance to live the life of our dreams. Lottery tickets do nothing to help us save and create wealth, yet people buy them every week. Why? The lottery gives us the chance to dream big—to think about what life would be like without having to worry about money and work.

Right now, you have permission to think big. You are encouraged to dream like you have never dreamed before. This entire chapter is designed to help you do that and to help you get those thoughts on paper.

CREATIVE ORDER

This chapter will help you put on paper the random but important thoughts racing through your head. Be creative and open to all ideas. Think about your wants *and* needs, your goals *and* dreams. Do you want to retire at a certain age? Do you expect your son with special needs to live with you forever, or do you want him to live independently when he reaches a certain age? Do you plan to pay for college for other children, take care of aging parents, fund a full-time caregiver, or incorporate Medicaid funding into your life? Do you want to hike the Inca trail, attend a Super Bowl game, box a kangaroo, or visit the Louvre in Paris with the entire family?

There are lots of questions, big and small, that need to be asked. There are dreams to write down and worries to get out.

This "creative order" gives you the chance to think about

everything you desire before making commitments to any of it. It is a chance to get down on paper what you have been dreaming about, worrying about, feeling, and imagining over the past months and years. The thoughts we have sitting at a traffic light or in a moment of reflection in a shoe store have no direction or pattern. This first Building Block of Blueprints will change that and put you in position to make the most important of your dreams come true while reducing your anxiety about the future.

ONE HOUR CHANGES YOUR LIFE

Do you remember those days when you sat in the back of your family's car on a long drive? Or the times you were stuck in a class on a warm spring day and couldn't concentrate on the work in front of you? What did you do? You dreamed. You thought about your ideal life. At least that's what I did.

We don't do that so much as adults. We rush from work to the supermarket to home to bed. Often we enjoy each of those moments and appreciate them. Other times we are just rushing. In any case, we are not spending time with our eyes closed, thinking about the best of all possible worlds and all the things we wish to do in life.

The thoughts, whims, and imaginations of the mind have unbelievable power if directed, focused, and harnessed into the right kinds of actions. Steve Jobs used his vision to create the iPhone, iPad, and iTunes. Jack Canfield put his to work to sell hundreds of millions of books around the world that offered a little "chicken soup for the soul." The Wright Brothers used theirs to initiate the age of flying.

This book does not ask that you invent the next "big thing." You are being given an instruction book on how to begin to change your family history for the better and to ensure the best possible chance for your family member with special needs to live a fulfilling life. To do that, you need a clear understanding, a clear mental picture, of what that life is like today and what you want it to be in the years to come.

Throughout this book, you will have exercises to help you move forward through the Blueprints process. Each exercise will direct you to the name of a checklist or worksheet that you can find in the Appendix section of the book.

Your first exercise is to free some space in your day and find a location—at your desk, on your front porch, or anyplace you can close your eyes and dream.

1. Carve out one hour to get started. An hour. Think about how much time passes each week in which you cannot remember what you did. This hour can come from getting up early one day, taking your lunch break in a private place where you can think, or shutting down the TV early.

2. Determine where you will spend your hour dreaming and jotting down your notes.

3. Make a date with yourself to dream, and be ready to record those dreams.

 Worksheet: Find Time to Dream

1. Decide on a time in the next week during which you will give yourself one hour of dream time. Choose a date and an exact time of day.

2. Determine the best location. I like to be outside to get my mind working on new and big ideas.

3. Find a small notebook or something to use for writing down your dream goals.

Seems easy enough, doesn't it? You wrote down three simple commitments: a day of the week, a time of day, and a location.

I worked with a coach many years ago who focused his clients on the importance of having a daily routine or ritual. He talked me through a simple exercise similar to the one above: find a place, specify a time, and do it every day. That's how I started, and I continue to follow this routine on a regular basis. My routine gives me time to relax, think through important issues, and focus on the meaningful outcomes I want in life.

You have now taken the single most important step in changing your financial life.

This is a book about special-needs planning; it will show you how to protect government benefits, save for future needs, and help create the wealth and income you need today and for the future. Like any good building project, the starting point for this one is in the planning and sketching. The building part—the foundation, frame, roof, and finishes—all of that comes later.

The most common reaction of people I meet with in my office is that of relief—before we have even started the process of building and putting the key elements in place. At first, this surprised me. I did not think that a one-hour meeting could make such an impact. But I learned that the one-hour meeting is often the first time families have given thought or voice to their concerns, worries, plans, and dreams. In one hour, we can often sketch out goals and help families understand that there are resources available to help them build the life they desire. Their relief comes in taking that first step toward putting plans in place to protect their family member with special needs and to create financial stability in their lives.

Most likely, you have a small sense of that in making this first decision. Your feelings of relief and your excitement about the future will only increase as you follow the Blueprints process to decide what you want and as you take the key actions toward making those desires happen.

COULDN'T DECIDE?

Some of you have not made the decision to take one hour to think about your dreams and goals yet.

Maybe you want to read the whole book first. Okay, do that. Just remember to come back to this step; avoid the temptation to jump into the parts you think you want to do first. Remember the concept: you need to have a set of plans in place before you can start building. Most of the people I meet with in my office or at speaking engagements have some of the Building Blocks in place, but they lack a plan that brings everything together. They may have a trust, a retirement plan, or some life insurance, but none of it is coordinated. This is like having a roof, a foundation, and kitchen counters all scattered around a building site. Each may be attractive and well-built built in and of itself, but none are useful if not coordinated and placed in the right order so that together they meet your needs.

Maybe fear is stopping you from committing to that hour of dreaming and planning. The fear may be based on many things. Maybe you're afraid of making a wrong decision. Maybe you're afraid to change the little voice in your head that says you do not deserve the life you want (a fear more common than it should be). Maybe you find that thinking about money, legal issues, and planning for the future creates anxiety that is easier avoided.

Planning may seem complex; the fear of the complex stops people from starting. Blueprints helps break down the planning into simple steps.

Maybe you can't move forward due to feelings of pain and sadness. Life with a person with special needs brings these feelings out for many of us at different times. I have seen my daughter's peers not include her in certain social activities from an early age. I look to her future years and wonder who her friends will be and if she will be given a chance at having a rich, fulfilling, and warm social life. She brings so many great traits to her peers through her humor, exuberance, and joy, but will others see it the same way I do—especially as her peer group goes through middle school?

What are my choices? I can choose to hold on to these fears, or I can decide to embrace the parts of life that make my daughter happy and that make me feel fulfilled. I choose to focus on the positive and to believe that she'll make friends and find her way.

Remember, the quality of life for your family member with special needs depends on you taking positive steps to make the most of his future. In reading this book, you're taking a step toward changing and improving life for you and your family. Eventually, you can change the way you feel about the future, and you can set each member of your family on a path toward achievable goals.

Some of you will need to put this book down and come back to it, as the future seems too difficult to imagine. If so, pick up the phone and find counselors, therapists, spiritual advisers, or friends and family who can help you move to a place where you can begin to embrace building a future for your family.

COMMIT TO A TIME AND PLACE

Put this on your calendar now—on your Outlook calendar, in your Day-Timer, on a note on your refrigerator, or in your phone. This meeting with yourself is more important than any other last-minute item that comes up, so make sure you are committed to the time. Tell the lunch group that meets every Friday you won't be joining them this week. Tell the soccer coach you won't be hanging around for practice at your usual spot on the sidelines. Don't sit at the physical therapy office talking with other parents or reading

People and *Oprah* magazines. Change your behavior this one time, and use that time to sit outside, in a local coffee shop, or anywhere else where you can think about the next steps in designing a plan for your family.

Are you a person who thinks most clearly in the morning before the rest of the house awakes? Do you prefer to get some exercise first to clear your head? Do you need to get breakfast made and people out the door before finding time? We each have a best time when we feel awake, ready to handle new ideas, and have few interruptions.

The place is important. You cannot stay in your office, where you will be disturbed by ringing phones and well-meaning colleagues who just "have to" talk to you right now, even though you've closed the door and cleared your schedule. You cannot stay at home if you are tempted to find things to do other than sit and think. It helps to find a place where you can think new thoughts and ideas rather than a place that supports everything you have been doing up to now—especially if you think you need to make significant changes. Many of you are working on new plans or thinking through your plans in a comprehensive way for the first time. You may need to make a break from past behaviors and thought patterns.

A few years ago, I needed a new place to think through the plans for my family. I found a bench in a local park where I went go before my run. This bench, which is hidden from nearby walkways by shrubs and a small stone wall, still has an open view of the Rocky Mountains. When I finished thinking through a few aspects of my planning, I headed off for my regular run through the park. The outdoors—with its birds, mountains, and nature—helped me open my mind and got me out of the usual routine of home and office. It was a place free of radios, televisions, traffic, computers, books, and anything else that would be distracting.

CREATE A DREAMLIST

At first, my dream and planning sessions were done where I did not have anything to write with. I thought my imagination could run free while running or sitting before I began my run. I did this a few times before realizing that I needed to get my ideas on paper and then organized in a way that I could turn some of those thoughts and dreams into reality.

Eventually, I turned this thought process into my personal financial plan and into a list of the top one hundred things I want to have, see, and experience in life. I wrote out what I would like for my children and the gifts I hoped to be able to give them.

There's a lot of variety to my DreamList. I have income goals based on the life I want to live and how much income I will need to do that.

I have travel dreams on the list. I lived in London and Taipei on a student's budget during college. I want to see other parts of the world, like India and Tibet, and to spend time vacationing in Hawaii.

My DreamList includes wishes for each of my children—like having my daughter with Down syndrome become a reader and finding ways for her to live as independently as possible. My goals include saving for my other children to help them have the best education and life experiences possible. They include eating in some of the world's best restaurants, spending time with family, and so many of the other things I want to do in life. Most of my wish-list items are experiences I wish to have or have again. Other people I work with include things they want to have, such as cars, boats, houses, or pieces of art.

Holding a dream session and writing down the results are the first steps toward building the life you want for yourself and your family member with special needs. It seems unlikely that this one action—writing your goals on paper—could make much of a difference, but it does. After all, you have been walking around for years at this point just thinking about all the things you want in life. The list gives you a way to measure and celebrate your progress and helps you stay accountable to yourself.

This list will be important as you move through this book and work through the Building Blocks. You will come back to it as you read more and do more of the exercises. Most of your list will not be achievable without building the strong legal and financial foundation you need to support your goals, but these will be discussed as we move through the Building Blocks.

Many of you likely have career or employment goals on your list. You may need to work on these simultaneously with your special-needs legal and financial planning to be able to finish all the Building Blocks. Your passion and desire to create the best life possible for you and your family member with special needs will help you increase your income and further your career as well.

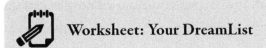 **Worksheet: Your DreamList**

KEY VALUES FOR YOUR FAMILY

In addition to your list of dreams, you will now write a list of key values. Again, you may be asking yourself, "What does this have to do with financial and legal planning? How does this help me save and invest for the future or get out of debt?"

Financial planning can look simple on paper. You spend less than you earn, save and invest the extra, and create a degree of wealth in the future.

Unfortunately, many people struggle with the basics of spending less than they earn and with saving for the future. There are many reasons for this. Some families do not practice good money management and pass those poor habits along to their children. Children of smokers are more likely to smoke than the rest of the population; the same is true with money habits. Children of savers tend to be savers. We tend to follow the path of our parents and those around us.

In addition, we live in a consumer culture where we are bombarded every day with messages to spend, spend, spend. These messages come in ads at sporting events, during newscasts, in email messages, on Facebook accounts, and in radio commercials. Stores advertise special promotions and sales that will not last, so we are told to spend today to take advantage of them. There is always a good deal if we buy now. Hardly any advertising messages tell us to put our money away for a rainy day or to hold on to a part of our paycheck for retirement. These concepts just don't seem as sexy for marketers. Benjamin Franklin's saying, "A penny saved is a penny earned," just can't be heard over the noise of "There's a special in aisle four!"

How do you combat the noise and relentless pull of those looking to separate you from your money? Making your list of life events and dreams is your first step.

Personal values do not usually make it into the conversations we have about money. We tend to think of money as something separate from personal values. Think about it, though. You may value providing a stable, loving household for your spouse and children, yet you have a mortgage that is too expensive or live on a street so busy you cannot sleep well or play in the front yard. There are social pressures at work when you make purchases that conflict with your stated purposes and values.

Most of us have not spent time thinking about or writing down our key values. This list may overlap in some ways with your DreamList. For example, you may have written that you want to live in a certain kind of house. Why is this? For me, home is the base of operations for a fun, exciting, stable life for my family. It is a place to create memories. It is a place to give my children a platform from which they can go into the world, knowing they have a loving family behind them and, ideally, a place to come back to when needed. We laugh at our kitchen table, play ball in the yard, and watch birds eat from the feeder on the porch. The value of having the right house for my family is lived every day we are together. Other families feel differently about their homes. For example, military families move every few years, and the feelings of home are created in different ways than for my family. These families may value adventure and new surroundings and show it in unique and personal ways.

I moved into the house in which I now live about a year before writing this book. The process of looking for a new home was a long one. I looked at houses of different sizes, on different streets, with different configurations, and in different price ranges. The goal was to buy a house I could make into a home and live in for many, many years. My value system helped me choose a great house in a great neighborhood. My values include high education expectations for all my children, the ability to easily enjoy the outdoors, family time that enriches each member of the family, and more. My home has a kitchen where we spend lots of time together, with an eating nook that makes it easy to go outside. We have enough room for each person but not so much that we get lost looking for each other. My home supports the way I want to live and my hopes for a family that grows to enjoy each other's company over time.

Over time, your personal value system will help you make the right decisions more often than not.

One of my clients was approached about investing in a private business. Most private businesses in the United States fail within the first five years. Still, there are times where it can make sense to invest in a new and growing business—if you do your homework, understand the risks, trust the people involved, and have enough of these types of investments so that when one or two fail, you have diversified your risk. My friend and client asked to me help him understand the investment and to read through the prospectus and other business information provided as part of the offering.

As we discussed how to begin looking at the investment, we first discussed his goals and values in life. The first question I asked him was, "Can you afford to lose the amount you would invest?" His answer was yes. My second question was, "How would you feel about losing the money invested?" His answer to that question was very different. He felt that the loss would matter, as it would stop him from accomplishing other, more important goals. The investment itself did not cross his goals; it was the use of the money that could be put toward other goals that were more important. In his case, reducing debt and putting money toward college education were more important to him. The discussion changed from "Will I make money and when?" to "Will I be better able to care for my family if I do not make this investment?"

Your values will help you make decisions that reduce stress, increase joy, and enable you to feel good all at the same time.

 Worksheet: Clarify Your Values

PERSONAL STRENGTHS

The first Building Block includes taking time to consider all you appreciate in your life today. It consists of two separate parts—strengths and appreciations.

First, you will build a personal inventory of your strengths and positive characteristics. Next, you will write down what you appreciate about the world you live in and the many ways you appreciate your family member with special needs.

Parents, spouses, siblings, and others who care for family members or friends with special needs have a deep reservoir of experience to draw from throughout the Blueprints process. We have learned compassion in new and unique ways. We have a degree of patience (often tested) deeper and stronger than those with typical family members. We have faced difficult times and come through intact.

Knowing your strengths and positive traits will help you should you encounter difficulty in working through the Building Blocks. Financial planning, investing, and creating the best life for yourself and your family do not happen all at once. It is not an event where you can buy a ticket, show up, enjoy the event, and then go home.

The Building Blocks are designed to move you from one strong stage of your financial and legal life to another. They build strength upon strength. You cannot have a strong estate plan without first having a vision of what you wish to have happen. You cannot build wealth and assets to care for your family member with special needs without a special-needs trust in place to preserve government benefits. You cannot save for retirement or fund a trust unless you first become free of most of your debt.

World-class athletes focus on their strengths and manage around their weaknesses. They identify their "game" and use that to their advantage. They are good at what they do because of their passion to practice and refine the parts of their sport that make them strong. Tiger Woods was known for going to practice at the driving range after he finished rounds during tournaments. He kept hitting golf balls, his key core athletic strength, to improve his game even as he was winning tournaments.

Identify your core strengths, as these will be important during the Blueprints process. I have taken multiple personality and work-profile exams over the years. I had the opportunity to go through a community leadership program at one of the country's top training centers for executives and management teams. This program included several personality and performance reviews designed to help those in the program know how we worked, how we interacted in groups, and how to excel. The program focused on helping us understand our strengths and learn to work from those strengths rather than just look at those parts of life that needed to be fixed. Once we understood and appreciated our strengths, we spent time understanding how they were different from others' strengths and how to work together to use the best of what we had and liked.

Strengths come in so many different forms. You may be strong in math or language skills, in fitness or musical activities, in following directions to a T or in finding new paths. Whatever your strengths are, write down as many of them as you can.

Circle three of the strengths you feel will be most important as you continue through the Blueprints process. All your strengths are like muscles you will continue to develop. Some of them will be critical for you to be aware of as you read the rest of this book and take your next step in creating the life you want for your family.

One of my strengths is persistence. Another is taking time for physical activity. Also, I like to read. These three help me stay focused, balanced, and moving forward even when faced with something difficult. Which three of your strengths are most important to you or do you think will help you the most over the next few months? Write these down on the personal strengths worksheet.

 Worksheet: Your Personal Strengths

APPRECIATION

My children have taught me much about life and they remind me so much of how exciting learning and growing can be.

My daughter with Down syndrome brings laughter, joy, and good times to my family in unexpected ways. When I was growing up, I did not have much experience with those with special needs. There were no other family members with disabilities, and my schooling took place at a time when people with learning challenges were separated into different classrooms.

At my daughter's birth, many new friends, families, and specialists came into my life. Many had the same message: my daughter would bring a new, enjoyable, and happy world to my family. It seemed like everyone was reading from the same script. Yes, there are difficult days—my daughter spent two weeks in the hospital as I wrote this book—yet those difficulties seem small when I step back and look at all she has brought to us.

The next step is one I took to heart: to write down ways I appreciate my daughter and how she has changed my life for the better.

Take the time now to write down ways you appreciate your family member with special needs. It may be his unique humor, life lessons you have learned (like patience or compassion), or new people you have met as a result of having this family member in your home.

Whatever things you appreciate, write down as many as you can.

 Worksheet: Appreciate Today

BIG STEP FORWARD

Congratulations! You have started the Blueprints process and gotten through the critical step that derails many families. You have taken the time to think about the future and gotten some thoughts and goals down on paper.

The first and most important part of Blueprints is putting together that initial vision of the future where you start to see what you want from life for yourself and each member of your family. At this point, you may not know which action steps to take to make that vision happen. That's not all: you may not yet believe in yourself enough to know that the power to make your vision come true lies within you.

Whatever you do, don't skip this first Building Block. It's the difference between success and failure. Blueprints planning takes time, energy, and commitment. It takes intensity, desire, and passion to change the life you have today into the life you want.

Once you've completed this Building Block, you now have in front of you the necessary and important tools to start building. The next Building Bock will help you organize those thoughts so you can determine which goals are most important to you and your family.

BUILDING BLOCK 2

Starting to Design

C an one word change your life? Can a three-letter word possibly point you in a new direction and keep you moving?

Researcher Carol Dweck demonstrates that how we think about what we are doing can support us in achieving our goals—or, conversely, can prevent us from attaining those goals. People with growth mindsets focus on developing themselves, working toward improving their future, and, most importantly, understanding that they can change.

Starting Blueprints puts you in new and unfamiliar territory. As you completed the first Building Block, you jumped into the unknown in a strategic and important way—though you won't see the results immediately. Each Building Block takes time to finish, and you must trust yourself and the process. There will be times when you think you are not getting there, when the work does not add up, when you think you are stuck.

Remember one simple word.

Yet.

With *yet*, you can keep the process alive. With *yet*, you can step back and think about what you have done so far and what you will achieve by learning new skills and finding the best way to protect your family.

The work of the first Building Block helps you when you are stuck, when you do not see that you are out of debt, when you don't have an estate plan in place, or when you have not saved money to fund a trust. The first Building Block helps you remember to say *yet*.

The DreamList, values and personal strengths you identified previously are the tools you'll need to keep your motivation and inspiration in front of you as you complete the rest of the Building Blocks. These give you a strong emotional connection and reasons to finish your plan. Inspiration, dedication, and determination are what you need to build the life you want.

The more you think about these key life goals and support those thoughts with positive emotions and action steps, the more likely you are to realize them.

The second Building Block helps you put your dreams in a format that will help you keep them with you as you complete the rest of the Building Blocks and move into the future.

MOTIVATION

The motivation for families like ours seems clear: to be able to care for a family member who will not be able to care for herself throughout life. We have the duty and obligation to provide care and support for our families, and this duty lasts our entire lifetime, as well as the lifetime of our family member with special needs. This does not mean we need to provide day-to-day care every single day; it *does* mean we need to build a structure and system to provide that care when and where needed.

For most families I meet with, this motivation comes from within. No one tells them to do this. It comes from the heart and from the love they develop as a result of having a family member with special needs.

Generations ago, families were counseled by the medical community to institutionalize their members with special needs. The assumption was that a person with Down syndrome, cerebral palsy, mental illness, or other developmental delays could not and should not live in the community. In today's world, the opposite is true. Families embrace these loved ones. But the special-needs issues change our long-term expectations and goals in ways different from our other family members, and they are goals we learn to love and accept.

You also must take care of yourself and find ways to live and enjoy life separate from the role of parent, sibling, or spouse. The list of life's dreams from the first Building Block must include all aspects of life that leave you feeling fulfilled, including travel, entertainment, family, spiritual, and career. These life goals become motivating forces that carry you through the Building Blocks.

You desire to increase the joy and happiness in your life while decreasing stress and worry. You can do that by following the Blueprints—by knowing you have taken care of basic legal and financial steps and outlined the dream life you wish to have.

VISION

As you plan and put the Building Blocks in place, you will hit hurdles and roadblocks. Some roadblocks may seem menacing and difficult to overcome—an example would be a medical crisis that requires you to spend all your emergency funds. Or the hurdle may take the form of a temptation, like the chance to buy an amazing piece of art or a new television set at an amazing discount at a time when that money should stay in your emergency fund.

Your vision of the future helps you stay on track by giving you the strength to clear these hurdles and to regroup after running into roadblocks. Your vision provides direction when you get lost. It acts as your roadmap to get you back on track if you take a side road.

The DreamList and the other tools in this book will help you keep your most important goals alive and in front of you. They will keep that vision alive as you grow, adapt, and gain new strengths when it comes to saving, investing, caring for your family, and enjoying life's offerings.

SPEED AND ENDURANCE

Financial planning, getting out of debt, creating assets, and forming an estate plan—some of the important Building Blocks in your plan—take a mix of speed and endurance.

Many of the tasks of the Blueprint planning process are simple, and some of the Building Blocks can be finished quickly. Your foundation, the special-needs trust and estate plan, can be finished within a few weeks. Most people can get their starter emergency fund in place quickly once they choose to focus on it. Collecting your important documents in a binder takes little time.

Other tasks involved in the process must be worked on regularly over a period of time. For example, your trust will be funded decades from now, and you will be putting money away each month for years. In a similar way, growing your retirement savings and other investments take time.

The dollars you put away for retirement or to fund a trust may appear insignificant at first, but over the years, these small amounts add up until eventually you see how sizable they are. You cannot take a few years off from these types of savings—you need to have the patience and endurance to let time and investments work for you.

NAVIGATION

Your vision acts as your navigation system; it keeps you moving through the Building Blocks and gets you back on track when you take a wrong turn. Your emotional connection to that vision will help you make the right decisions as you move forward.

One couple I work with had a date circled on the calendar by which they planned to pay off their mortgage: 12/12/12. It was easy to remember. They had decided a few years earlier to pay off all their debts, including their mortgage, and then get serious about retirement savings. They wanted less stress and more enjoyment out of life; their debts had become a burden, and it was time for those debts to be eliminated.

We met about one year before the 12/12/12 target date for an annual review, and I asked how it was going. The husband and wife were very excited about how close they were to getting out of debt. They talked about the sacrifices they had made to get to this point and how it was worth all they'd had to do. With less than a year to go, they were excited about being done, and they were proud of their hard work. This date and their commitment to change their lives kept them focused and on track.

They had a vision for their financial future that included a major goal on 12/12/12—paying off all debt. They connected to this event, as it would help them live a less stressful life when they didn't owe a single cent to anyone. They also looked forward to having even less financial stress, as they could now build their assets to provide for a comfortable retirement.

DESIGN YOUR DREAM LIFE

In this chapter, you'll start to design the plan. You have created the first Building Block by identifying your dreams. With Building Block 2, you will organize the ideas, thoughts, and notes you've written down as a foundation on which to formulate your dreams.

The more you have written and organized your goals, the easier it will be when you start the "building" phases of your special-needs planning. You will meet with an attorney, financial adviser, CPA, and nonprofit program directors as you formulate this plan. You will also talk to family and friends about it. Each person you speak with along the way will help you turn your visions of the future into a living, working reality.

Your goals and plan don't have to be so detailed or perfect at this stage that there is no room for change.

But when you do meet with an attorney or financial planner, you want to be ready with some basic information, and this chapter will help you prepare for that. The attorney and financial planner is going to ask you about your goals, about your financial status, about your entire family, and about some of the dreams you have for the future.

REVIEW YOUR DREAM SHEET

Look at your notes from Building Block 1 where you wrote down your life's dreams and goals. It's time to organize your list so you know which goals to work on first and which are most important in several different categories.

To get started, take out a new sheet of paper or use the Map My Dreams worksheet.

 Worksheet: Map My Dreams

There are six main sections on the Map My Dreams worksheet: Family, Finances, Career, Special Needs, Recharge/Play/Spirituality, and Rewards.

Your DreamList from Building Block 1 will have captured your thoughts but in no particular order. Ideally, you did not censor your list in any way; instead, you should have written down each and every dream, goal, and wish. Some dreams may have felt silly or insignificant; others too big or impossible. If you didn't write them all down, go back and do that now. It will put you in touch with important emotions and thoughts waiting to be let out and lived.

In this Building Block, you're going to order your thoughts so you can tackle the most important ones first. As you look at the categories below, you'll find that some goals may fit into several categories; in that case, choose the category that is most meaningful or makes the most sense to you.

Family Goals. Family goals may be immediate or long term. You may want to send your children to private school next year, move into a house that better suits your family's needs, attend a reunion, reduce conflict between family members, or increase the enjoyment you have today (even if you have three teenagers). My family goals include sending my children to camps and colleges and helping them become successful, independent adults.

Financial Goals. Financial goals can include things like getting out of debt, saving for retirement, building emergency funds, and investing for future needs. They may also include a specific net-worth goal, saving for a down payment on a house, or funding travel.

Career Goals. Do you need to increase your income or find a job better suited to your talents and interests? If these are on the list, write them in the career area. Maybe you want to move up the ladder at your current job, earn more with your current employer, or even change careers. These are examples of what fall into the career area.

Special-Needs Goals. This category will have unique goals and other goals that may overlap with others. A family goal for me is to have my children become independent, successful adults. This is true for my two typical children and for my daughter with Down syndrome. However, the goal looks different in some ways and has a different timeline for my daughter with Down syndrome. A different level of effort will be needed as she becomes an adult. It will require research of supporting nonprofit organizations, finding housing and employment, and working with her to develop the skills she will need to cook, shop, commute, and live her daily life. This goal, then, is one that's repeated in the Family Goals section but that must also be delineated here because of the extra requirements.

Recharge/Play/Spirituality Goals. Life is best lived when we take care of ourselves. For many, this means having a higher purpose and celebrating God or taking time for reflection. Travel, vacations, exercise, yoga, art classes, hobbies, and anything else we do to take care of our minds, bodies, and emotions falls into this area. This category often has the most number of goals in it, as it is easy to write down how we want to spend our time.

Rewards Goals. Some of my life goals feel like rewards. They are purchases I want to make, trips I want to take, or experiences I want to have that will come once I have hit certain milestones in life. Write these down. Celebrations are a big part of success in planning.

Blueprints Goals. Add the following to your Map My Dreams worksheet. These are Blueprints goals that must happen and cannot be left off your goals and dreams worksheets.

- Hire an attorney to draft a will with special-needs trust provisions.
- Eliminate debt.
- Build emergency funds.

- Start retirement savings.
- Make a plan to fund a special-needs trust.

ORDER OF IMPORTANCE

Your list may have ten, fifty, or a hundred different lines on it. There is no way to work on all of them at once, and some are clearly more important than others.

Once you have separated the items on your DreamList into different categories, you will likely notice recurring themes, desires, and goals. You will also notice that some of these goals—like retiring comfortably—are years in the future. Others will have shorter timeframes. Things like changing jobs, paying off student loans, or buying a new wheelchair may be much more immediate.

So often, the reaction is to go straight to work on the short-term goals that seem like they can be achieved right away. Put the brakes on for a second! Take a step back from your wallet. The purpose of this chapter is to help you focus on the most important goals, the ones that will truly help you feel comfort and peace in regard to the future. Taking steps toward your important goals will let you sleep better at night and look toward the future in a different way.

You are reading this book to gain control over the future—to make decisions that will let you live the life you want and provide the best quality of life for you and each member of your family. A degree of patience is needed to make that happen.

Now, take your list and a new piece of paper. Write down your top ten goals in order of priority and importance.

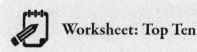 **Worksheet: Top Ten**

One of my goals is to eat in the best restaurant on each continent at some point in my life. I like restaurants, and I am amazed at how interesting dishes can be prepared by brilliant, artistic chefs making the most of locally sourced foods. A plate from a great chef can look like a piece of art, taste like nothing else, and provide me with a memory that lasts a lifetime. I still remember the food, the setting, and the great time I had with family eating at a restaurant called L'Ami Louis in Paris when I was in my early twenties. I'm hungry just thinking about how good it was.

Still, when I look at my list, I see other life goals that stand out as more important and that require my immediate attention. My children will go to college, and I want to pay for their education. My daughter with Down syndrome will need additional funds for transportation, health, and activities, and I will need to save for her over time. As I was writing my list, one of my goals was to write this book and get it published, which has taken time from some of my more fun and entertaining goals. That's an example of how the more important goals have pushed some of the more fun goals to the background for now.

This does not mean that none of my fun goals is happening. The prioritized list helps provide focus for my most important goals and a guide for balancing decisions when I need to choose between one option or another. I did eat in a restaurant owned and run by one of the "Iron Chefs" last year on a client visit in California. I was able to combine my current work goals with my life dream of fine dining without feeling like I'd made a bad decision in either case.

Your list will prove helpful in many situations as you begin to work with key people and organizations toward your goals for your family member with special needs and for yourself.

At some point along the way, you will work with a financial planner/investment adviser, lawyer, and accountant. You will consider which nonprofit organizations can help your family, who should act as guardian, and how to manage a trust with key advisory members. You will communicate your hopes and wishes to other family members, spiritual leaders, teachers, school administrators, and other community members. You will not share every item on the list with every person, of course, but having the list will help you see how certain people can act as resources to help you accomplish other goals. For example, a financial planner can help you find the leading charitable organizations with which you can work.

My list has other goals that can be done now—like run a half marathon, read a book per month, and write a book. It has other goals that will have to come later as my financial life catches up to my DreamList.

Your list will include things you can and need to do now, things you can work on today, and things that can happen only after you have a strong foundation in place. You will have important and high-priority goals that will have to wait until you have the time and money to do something about them. Life drags us in the direction of whatever screams loudest. The list you put together gives you the power to act on those aspects of life that are most important and meaningful to you.

Creating priorities leads to significant change and an improved quality of life. Priorities help you create the intention and focus you need to go through difficult times. The sense of purpose created by focusing on your priorities keeps you motivated and on track.

TIMELINE OF NEEDS

As you review your goals, you'll realize that some will take place on a timeline that happens whether you are ready or not. Our children become adults at age eighteen according to Social Security and most laws. You may have to establish a guardianship for your family member with special needs at this age. Some families need to replace medical equipment on a set schedule. A surgery may have to take place to improve health, and you may be able to anticipate such surgery.

You also may set dates on your goal sheet for retirement, house projects, family trips, and other life events. College education starts according to your children's ages. These dates need to be understood so you can be emotionally, legally, and financially prepared.

KEEP YOUR GOALS ALIVE AND PRESENT, AND BE PASSIONATE ABOUT THEM

There are a number of ways to keep your goals alive and present in your life. You can write your most important goals on note cards and look at them every day as you wake up or go to bed. You can put the list on your refrigerator. I take time every day to sit and think about my goals and how excited and happy I will be when I see progress. Put your goals in the most positive light possible and think about how good you will feel when you reach a milestone.

CELEBRATE!

Blueprints is designed to bring you and your family joy and peace of mind. You are doing important work in areas you may not feel comfortable in or about which you may have some guilt. Remember the importance of what you're doing. Enjoy the process as much as possible and celebrate each accomplishment, Building Block, and personal milestone along the way.

These celebrations can be small or large, depending on the effort you've put in and the goal you have reached. For some people, finishing Building Block 3 (Taking Stock) is a big step, as organizing important papers may take weeks. For others, the biggest celebration will be when they are out of debt or have a certain amount saved for retirement.

Some celebrations may be small, but they are still important. Even finding one hour of time each week to work on the Building Blocks is an important step that should be celebrated. This celebration could involve enjoying a cup of coffee during that time or just taking a few moments to appreciate how good it feels to have an hour to yourself.

Whatever it is for you, celebrate any progress you make. Recognize both your efforts and accomplishments, and think about how much better your life will be for you and your family once you have a strong legal and financial plan in place.

 Worksheet: Celebrations and Rewards

You now have the elements of your design in place. You have identified the most important goals for you and your family. You have mapped those goals into different categories so you can work on different parts of your life as you build a financially secure foundation for your family.

This book is designed to move you toward having foundational legal and financial Building Blocks in place, enabling you to create the life you've always dreamed of living. The next two Building Blocks can be completed within thirty days. You'll feel an enormous sense of relief when you finish them.

The financial Building Blocks take longer. Getting out of debt requires energy, commitment, and focus. You have your motivation now—creating security for your family and living the life of your dreams. The Dreamsheets will keep you excited about the future waiting for you.

BUILDING BLOCK 3

Taking Stock

Having completed the first two Building Blocks, you are now focused on your key life goals. But you you're still not ready to start the actual building process.

That doesn't mean you're stalled, by any means. Every construction project starts before a hammer ever touches a nail. It begins with a vision of the future. It continues with identifying and collecting any resources you have and bringing them together.

A hailstorm recently hit my neighborhood. Weeks after the storm, trucks delivered wood, sheeting, and nails to the houses that needed new roofs. Dumpsters were parked under the edges of the roof. Work did not start right away, even though the materials had been delivered.

At my house, the person in charge of the job came by to check that all the materials were there; he then scheduled a time to start the work. Once the crew started, the work itself did not take long. The old roof was off in a day, and the new materials were put in place in a few more days. The work went smoothly because the vision of the job was clear and all the materials were organized before the job actually got underway.

Taking Stock is the Building Block where you organize the financial and legal aspects of your life to prepare for the building of your Blueprints plan.

The first two Building Blocks—Dreaming About Your Future and Starting to Design—helped you understand what you want from life and where you want your family to be in the future. Before you start working to get there, you need to have a clear understanding of your current resources. You need to know if you have enough money saved for retirement, to fund a trust, or to take a trip to Disneyland next year. The professionals you work with will need reports to know how to take the next steps.

Taking Stock shows you how to organize the financial and legal aspects of your life. Once you've compiled all the necessary materials, you'll begin writing down important information regarding them on a couple of simple worksheets—the balance sheet and income statement.

The balance sheet and income statement let you know what tools you have to work with and any barricades you may face. As you progress through the Building Blocks, these worksheets will help you chart your financial progress.

BUILDING MATERIALS

It's time to organize your financial and legal documents. The word *organize* may drive fear into your heart. I might as well ask you to fly to the moon, speak to a crowd of rocket scientists about how liftoff works, or walk a tightrope across Niagara Falls. If you feel this way, know that I am only asking you to organize on a temporary basis. You have gotten this far with whatever organizational system (or not) works for you. You do not need to change everything before you can work on the Building Blocks of your special-needs plan.

Or you may feel the opposite: you may look at this simple step and feel eager to get it done—or maybe you've even had it done for years. If so, this chapter will validate how important it is to have this information ready.

By the time you finish this Building Block, you will have a clear picture of your financial status and have the documents ready to get your legal work finished. You will start making progress on creating the future you envision for yourself and your family.

FINANCIAL FLOATERS AND RECORD KEEPERS

If you are married or living with someone, it's likely that one of you manages the day-to-day bookkeeping and collects all the appropriate records. The other one probably floats in and out.

One of you likes to open the mail, download account information, and balance the checkbook—that's the Record Keeper. The other is more spontaneous and prefers to keep the house alive and filled with energy—that's the Financial Floater. One of you cannot live without a sense of order; the other cannot live without spontaneity.

It's okay that the household consists of these two types of people. But it's also important that each person in the relationship commit to planning, envisioning the future, and putting time and energy into making their dreams come true.

While each partner has an important role to play, this chapter is for the Record Keeper in your family. The Record Keeper knows where to find the will, the passcodes for each financial account, and maintains a file that contains the bills, statements, and other financial documents.

If you are the Financial Floater, then turn the work of this Building Block over to the Record Keeper. This does not mean you can ignore it forever; just let the Record Keeper take the checklist and get everything together for now. Let the Record Keeper fill out the worksheets in this Building Block.

Once the Record Keeper is done, sit down together to review the worksheets and go through the documents. Each of you needs to know your current legal and financial status. You will each need to be committed to the Blueprints process and to working together to improve your financial life.

DATA GATHERING

One of my clients has a table in her house where she keeps all her mail, including her financial statements and other important documents. This "system" has worked well for a period of time. When she first consulted me, I asked her for the documents we would need for planning—documents her attorney would also need. Thanks to her "system," she had everything she needed in one place. Unfortunately, that table was piled high from end to end. It took some time—longer than it should have—but we got everything together and moved the plan forward. Once we had everything, the table went back to the way it was, useful for holding a lot of stuff that was not going to be needed on a day-to-day basis. Her temporary organizational efforts enabled us to gather the key documents and start the next steps included in this Building Block.

The checklist in this section provides a guide to the types of information financial planners and estate attorneys need to be able to help you. At my office, when we work with people on financial plans, our first few meetings usually go in one of two directions. One is where people have a pretty good idea of their financial status and can either provide documents or answer questions about the value of their house, size of the mortgage, how much they earn and save each year, and more. These people are ready to plan, move forward, and make changes that ensure stability, provide peace of mind, and offer hope in achieving future goals.

The other direction is where people feel like they should plan but are not really committed to it. They sit with me because they know they should, not because they want to. They are not prepared and are looking for the exit. Sometimes these meetings end up going well, and the people leave ready to move forward. More often than not, once these people leave our office, they do not take the important steps that will start to pay off for them. A year later, they are in the same place—and they wonder what happened.

You don't want to be in the same place one year from now. The quality of life and the future of your family member with special needs cannot be left to chance.

Gathering the information on the checklist is usually quite simple. Within several hours this week, you can have your documents together.

The following checklist will help you determine what documents to gather for the initial meetings you'll have with key professionals, each of whom will use this information in different ways. The financial adviser, for example, will look at your income statement and balance sheet to understand your current resources and figure out how to help you build your resources for the future. The attorney will need to review these documents so she can start a discussion with you about how best to distribute your assets. The financial planner will help identify which assets to use to fund a trust. The CPA will work to identify any tax issues that may apply and develop strategies to help reduce taxes.

Some people's financial lives are simple—they may own a house or perhaps have retirement and savings accounts. Others have complex financial lives that include existing trusts, business interests, multiple properties, and more. Your legal and financial planning should incorporate all aspects of your life. But first you need to know what they are.

This Building Block starts with your gathering the following documents. Get them out now.

Building Block 3 Checklist

- ☐ Bank account or credit-union account statements
- ☐ Investment account statements
- ☐ Individual retirement accounts and employer retirement account statements, including 401(k) and 403(b) accounts
- ☐ Pension estimates and values
- ☐ Annuity statements
- ☐ Life-insurance policy information (coverage-summary pages, recent statement, and/or last invoices)
- ☐ Current real-estate values (include estimate of purchase dates)
- ☐ Mortgage information—include current balance, interest rate, payment amount, number of years, and start date
- ☐ Credit-card statements
- ☐ Student-loan statements
- ☐ Homeowner's-insurance and car-insurance policy declaration pages
- ☐ List of significant personal property, such as automobiles, boats, jewelry
- ☐ Disability-insurance policy page and last invoice

☐ Long-term care insurance policy page and last invoice

☐ Buy/sell agreements

☐ Business valuations

☐ Stock-option plan information

☐ Deferred-compensation contracts

☐ Social Security annual statement

☐ Collectibles information, such as coins, art, and antiques, including estimated values

☐ Other

 Worksheet: Financial Checklist

This checklist includes items we're all familiar with, like checking and savings accounts, credit cards, homeowner's insurance, and the other basic financial tools needed to live in today's world. Most of us are familiar with the other financial items listed here, such as retirement plans and IRA accounts, mortgages, home values, and key information from life-insurance policies.

Even though you may be familiar with these documents, special-needs planning requires you to look at your balance sheet in different ways than typical families do. An asset as simple as a house owned by a husband and wife can become complicated in the world of special-needs planning. This important asset for a typical family will be used for many years and sold at some point when the owners wish to downsize or need to sell the home to pay for retirement or assisted-care facility expenses. Sometimes a person lives in a home her whole life and her family sells it when she dies. Families who have members with special needs must look at the home (and other assets) in a completely different way.

Many of my clients hope that when they die, their sons and daughters with special needs will be able to stay in the family's home. Other times, the family home is the main asset used to fund a special-needs trust, an asset to be used long after the owner passes away.

The checklist is meant to include items we've seen as we've worked with families of many different backgrounds. Naturally, not everyone will have all the assets on the checklist (and some may have assets not included). For example, a business owner will need to determine the value of his company in the planning work we do and will need to include that in the estate plan he develops with his lawyer. Often, a person who owns a business has most of his net worth wrapped up in the business.

Other families have money tied up in trusts even before they consider special-needs planning. In some states, like California, many people have their significant assets in trusts because both the time and expense of probate are high. In Colorado, where I live, trusts are less common, as probate is a fairly simple and inexpensive process.

Trusts are used by some families to pass along family wealth or to shift assets and income to different generations. They can also be used to protect family assets from lawsuits. Sometimes these trusts conflict with special-needs planning and must be reviewed as part of the overall process.

SCORECARDS AND STATS

On any given day you can hop online, turn on the TV, or open the newspaper and get a quick look at who won last night's baseball game: Yankees—2, Red Sox—1 (yes, I am a Yankees fan). The outcome of the game is easy to find.

Serious baseball fans can dig deeper if they wish. They can look at who hit home runs, which pitchers gave up runs, and who stole bases, had fielding errors, grounded out, flied out, or struck out. The details about the game go on and on. These stats have been part of baseball for generations and give fans a way to understand the game beyond the basic score.

The same can be said of financial planning and investing. You can take a detailed approach and examine your account's underlying investments, assets, liabilities, income, and future expectations. Or you can just look at the highlights, keeping it simple and know which numbers are important to you on any given day or in any given month or year—in essence, whether you're winning or losing more games.

If you prefer this second approach, take heart. You've already done the bulk of the work in gathering your most important financial documents. Next, you'll be able to consolidate all that information, keeping your financial life so simple you can review it on three pages.

These three pages detail your assets, liabilities, and income statement. They are the scorecard of your financial life. You can take one quick look at them and immediately know your standing in regard to your financial life—just like looking at the final score lets you know which team won the game.

BALANCE SHEET

Recently, I met with a client who has a brother with special needs. The brother with special needs is older than sixty, and their mother passed away a few years ago. Mom was a saver. She taught her children to save as well.

When my client came in for his review, I was curious about how his financial life had changed since we had been working together, so I decided to look back five years (from 2013). The previous five years had included one of the greatest collapses in the stock market in a hundred years. The Great Recession of 2008–2009 came close to beating the Great Depression in reducing portfolio values, creating unemployment, and resulting in financial uncertainty. I brought out my client's balance sheet, and we looked at his assets and liabilities.

So how did this client do? He had become a near-millionaire during this time. This can happen to you and to every other reader of this book. How? This man kept saving, stayed invested, and paid off his debts. He never had a big income, never played the lottery, and did not inherit his money. He saved, invested, and spent less than he earned his whole life.

We took a moment for congratulations. He had earned his comfort and success.

We would not have known the progress he made or even how well he had done unless we had worked out the numbers—his assets and liabilities—on a balance sheet.

Your balance sheet includes two sections. The first section is titled "Assets." The second section is titled "Liabilities."

Over time, you want to grow your assets and reduce your liabilities. The purpose of the balance sheet is to give you a quick snapshot of how you're doing. The more you have in assets and the less in liabilities, the more likely it is that you are on your way to being able to create a financial platform for your future needs and goals.

Imagine a life where you own everything outright. You do not owe the bank a dime on your mortgage. You do not have any payments for cars, boats, or credit cards. A future where you build wealth in this way is possible.

When people come to my office, we create a balance sheet and an income statement and start (or continue) working on a list of dreams and goals on a planning sheet. You've already started the planning sheet, your DreamList. By adding the balance sheet, we discover whether your financial life is keeping pace with your goals and whether you are moving in the right direction.

ASSETS

Assets are those things you own. Key assets include your home, retirement accounts, investment or brokerage accounts, artwork, gold bars, cars, jewelry, and antiques. The value of your business is an asset if you can sell it.

Assets work for you. They have the potential to grow in value and provide income or money to fund your goals.

Your assets will be viewed differently in some ways for estate planning and financial planning. You don't have to think about that at this stage. Simply write down any items that would have value if you were to sell them today.

Write down each asset or account: House, IRA, Spouse IRA, 529 plan for son, 529 plan for daughter, rental property, cars. Each asset will have its own line with a value and other information.

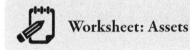 **Worksheet: Assets**

ASSET VALUES

For each item on the balance sheet, write its current value, or market value—the value of the asset today.

For some assets, the current market value is simple to find. For example, you can pull out a bank statement and know the value of that account. You could walk into the bank today and put that money in your hand if you needed to.

For other assets, it's more difficult to determine current market value. Take a house, for instance. Most of us know what we paid for the house we live in now. We do not always know what we could get for it if we put it on the market tomorrow. In many parts of the country, home prices lost significant value during the market downturn in 2008 and 2009. In some cases, those prices have recovered and surpassed prior market highs, while some markets or neighborhoods are taking longer to recover. The value of your home or any other hard-to-price asset should be a close estimate of what you would get if you sold that asset today (or during the next ninety days). This asset value is not what you want, need, or hope to get. It is what you can expect to get and get soon.

What follows is a short list of key assets and how to determine what values to put on the balance sheet.

Savings and Checking Accounts

These are the simplest assets to list. You just take out your last statement (or look it up online) and look for the number in the account. Savings and checking accounts do not include investments that fluctuate in value, so you know what you have in these.

Retirement Accounts

There may be one retirement account, like a 401(k), with your current job. Or you may have half a dozen—401(k)s, IRAs, Roth IRAs—with different employers or at different investment firms.

Finding the current market value of these types of accounts is usually as simple as it is for your checking account. Each month or each quarter you receive a statement by mail or email. Somewhere on the first two pages of that statement, you will see the current account value. Take the most recent statement and use that value for each of your retirement accounts.

Education Accounts

Families with children often have accounts to fund future educational needs. These are usually 529 plans, education IRAs, or UGMA/UTMA accounts. Get the most recent statement for each of these and write down the account value.

Investment Accounts

Your family may have investment accounts separate from retirement investments and checking accounts.

Investment accounts can hold many of the same assets you see in retirement accounts—money market funds, mutual funds, index funds, stocks, bonds, cash reserves, and more.

These accounts may have additional names to identify them—like a "revocable trust" or "TOD." Write these names down. Use the same method for investment accounts as you did for retirement accounts and savings: get a recent statement and use the current market value from that statement.

Trust Accounts

You may have inherited assets in a trust. Trusts can own the same financial assets as investment accounts, and they can also own cars, houses, real estate, business interests, and just about anything. Write down the current market value of the trust. This is simple if it holds one investment account. If your trust has complex holdings, you may need to create a separate balance sheet for it.

Houses

Typically, prices for houses and land do not change drastically from month to month. Fast-moving markets may see home prices change significantly every six months to a year. This happens more when interest rates are low or when there is some unusual event driving demand (like a new employer opening a big office in your town).

You probably have some idea of the value of your home based on informal market research. Many people stop at open houses or get fliers at properties for sale in their neighborhood. Online real estate pricing and data sites give a rough estimate but can be way off if your home is unique. You most likely have a general sense of whether homes have sold quickly or if homes are taking longer to sell. Some cities and counties do a great job of assessing for tax purposes and come close to current market values for homes.

Using all of this information, you can come up with a close estimate of the value of your home.

There are two other steps you can take to get a value on your home. You can call a real-estate agent who specializes in your neighborhood and ask that person to come to your home and give you a market estimate. Most agents do not mind doing this as they get a chance to talk with someone who may need real estate services in the future. Be respectful of the agent's time and let him or her know whether you plan to sell soon or not.

The other step involves paying for an appraisal. This is unnecessary at this point in the Blueprints process. You'll need an appraisal only if you refinance or take out a home-equity loan; you may also need one if you plan to gift the real estate in the near term. For estate and financial planning, a rough estimate of the value of your home is good enough for now.

Rental Properties

Putting a dollar amount on your rental property is similar to that on your residence if the rental is a single-family home or duplex. It is generally pretty easy to figure out what these would be worth if you were to sell them soon.

If your rental has four or more units, you may need to use a different formula to determine an asset value. If you recently purchased the property, it will be close to your purchase price. If you bought the property years ago, it is worth speaking with a real-estate agent who specializes in multifamily buildings to find out the current market value.

Business Interests

Write down the current market value of your business if you own one. Listing the current value of your business is likely the most difficult part of building your personal balance sheet.

You do have people to turn to for valuations if you own a business. You can call a business broker who works in your community or specializes in your industry—much like calling a real-estate agent for your home. These professionals use basic metrics common to business transactions and can help you think through how much you could sell your business for if you were to sell it today. You could also call an appraiser to get a value on your business. Many larger CPA firms have business appraisers you can hire to give you a more detailed analysis.

Most at-home businesses do not have a sale value. They make money for you today but do not have much tangible value to sell in the future.

No matter what the asset, remember to use its current market value. Do not use what you paid for it or what you wish it was worth. Also, do not deduct anything on the asset line for debts you owe against an asset. You will show all your debts in the next section of the balance sheet.

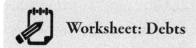 **Worksheet: Debts**

DEBTS (LIABILITIES)

Start listing your debts on a new piece of paper or at the bottom of the Blueprints balance sheet.

Your list of debts shows those companies, organizations, and people to whom you owe money. Debts show you borrowed money to buy something and have not yet paid that money back. You owe an interest rate on each of these debts, have a time period to pay it back, and have to make some sort of regular payment toward paying back the money you owe. All these factors will be captured on your personal balance sheet in the liabilities section.

If you have debts you cannot pay back, your financial life needs to change, and change dramatically. So many people today cannot make any progress toward living the life they want because they are paying for the life they already lived.

If this is you, the Blueprints balance sheet will help you take steps to get out of debt. So often the people we meet do not really understand how much debt they have and how much it costs them each month, let alone how to develop a strategy to get out of debt. The balance sheet asks you to list your debts, the amounts due each month, the interest rates, the terms of the loans, and the current balances.

Take a moment now and write down "getting out of debt" on your goals sheets if you have debt and have not yet established that as a goal. Write on your goals sheet that you will live a life free of debt in the future as well. You cannot make financial progress until you change your thinking on how you use your credit cards, car loans, school loans, loans from family, and every other type of loan out there except an affordable mortgage.

Most of my clients have debt on their house. This is the only type of debt that makes sense in your financial life. You have to live somewhere, and the mortgage payments on your home are usually less than the cost of renting. Your other debts are likely for things you bought long ago, most of which you cannot even remember. These debts do you no good now and were for things you could not afford at the time.

The bottom of the Blueprints balance sheet has several columns for you to track key information about your debts:

- Type of debt (mortgage on residence, college loan, credit card, car loan).
- Lender
- Amount owed
- Interest rate
- Monthly payment

Loans with fixed time periods like mortgages, college loans, and car loans will require you to write down other information, such as the start date of the loan and its term or the number of years until full payment is due.

Follow this form to develop a complete understanding of your overall debt plus your payments. What follows is a list of the liabilities you're likely to have.

Mortgage

A mortgage represents money you borrowed to buy a home. Mortgage debt usually has a term of repayment, usually fifteen or thirty years. You have an interest rate—likely somewhere between 4 and 8 percent. You make payments that consist of principal and interest; taxes and insurance are also usually bundled into your payment.

Mortgages are secured by your property. This means you can have your home or other real estate foreclosed on and taken by the lender if you do not make your regular payments.

Student Loans

Students take out loans so they can afford a college education, often with the expectation that it will improve their ability to earn a higher income. Unfortunately, too many people today have taken out student loans only to find they cannot earn enough to pay back the loans.

These loans typically carry a low interest rate, but graduates in the workforce should still focus on paying them down instead of spending money on their lifestyle. If you have a student loan, remember its purpose—it was taken out to give you the means to earn a higher degree of income. Once you start working, the loan debt does not help. It drags your financial life down. I have clients who still have student loans fifteen and twenty years out of school and who live under constant financial and personal stress from having to pay on those loans every month.

Credit Cards

Our society today seems built on the idea of spending today and figuring out how to pay for it tomorrow. That seems backward to me and is not the way my successful clients live. Write down each of your credit card accounts on the debt section of the balance sheet using the information from above. Include all credit cards, including store charge accounts.

Car Loans

Write down the amounts you owe for the cars you have purchased with a loan. This is a simple step now that you have the hang of this worksheet. Later we will see how much this loan could be worth if you used this money to put toward your own investments instead of being in debt to the bank.

Personal and Other Loans

Write down any personal loans you have with family members or friends and include the same information as with the other loans—length of the loan, interest rate, and other applicable information.

NET WORTH

You now have a sheet of paper with two sections—assets and debts. Total all the assets at the top. Total all the debts at the bottom. Subtract the debts from assets and you have your net worth.

Your net worth is a financial number that acts like a progress report on your financial life. A negative net worth indicates you are not building well and that you need to work differently to improve your financial life. A positive and growing net worth shows you're building a strong financial future to fund your life's goals.

Each year, you will expect your net worth to grow as you pay down debts, save money, and have the value of your assets increase. If your net worth does grow, you know you are making progress toward your goals. If it does not grow, take time to examine why.

INCOME STATEMENT

There is one more piece of financial information you'll need to write on a worksheet before you move to the next Building Block: your income statement. This shows your sources of income, how much you receive from each source, and in some cases how long you expect to receive this income.

Use a new piece of paper or the Blueprints Income Sources worksheet in the appendix.

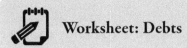

Worksheet: Debts

Write down each income source.

Some people have multiple income streams. You may have rental income or royalty income from something you created. In Colorado, some people receive income from oil or natural gas wells on their property. You may receive annuity payments from a settlement or annual gifts from family members.

Write down the income you receive from each source each month and total it for the whole year. Write down the pretax, or gross, amount and the amount you take home each month after taxes, insurance, and other deductions.

Whatever the source, get it down on paper. Using income to save is the greatest way to create the wealth and prosperity you need for retirement, to pay for future special-needs expenses, and to fund other dreams. If you understand your income today, you can be sure you are saving and investing enough of it for the future.

EMERGENCY PLANNING

Now that you've consolidated your financial life onto two simple documents, you should have a greater degree of clarity. But there's one final step you should take before finishing this Building Block: provide clarity to someone who may have to step into your shoes to navigate a crisis. You will want that person—your spouse, brother, sister, or best friend—to know who to call and where to look for bank records, investment accounts, and legal documents. Make life easier for the person who has to step into your shoes so that you can quickly make life as good as possible for your family member with special needs.

The emergency may be something harmless, such as having your return flight from a business trip delayed for twenty-four hours due to snow and ice. Or it could be something more serious, such as a health issue that leaves you in the hospital. Whatever it is, would you rather leave the care and well-being of your family member with special needs in the hands of someone who can quickly and easily take over, or with someone who has to spend hours searching through your house and who still might not find what is needed? What if that person needs to show proof that he has the legal power to make medical decisions or that there is health insurance so your son or daughter can access health care in an emergency room? Unnecessary delays can be easily avoided by investing a few minutes in organization today.

Take the following steps to save yourself time and stress. Organize your important documents and develop a simple system for handling the flood of paperwork that comes into your house each day. Have a place to file bank, retirement plan, and investment statements. You will want to add your legal documents to this emergency file once you have them (after Building Block 4). Make sure a copy of your health insurance and Medicaid information is there, too.

Here are a few basic steps:

Decide if you are a three-ring binder person or a hanging-file person. Create a separate file folder or section in the binder for each asset and liability on your balance sheet. Put labels on each folder or on each tab so the necessary information is easy to find.

Make a copy of each statement, or put the most recent statement in each section according to the tab. Add the following tabs as well:

- Balance sheet
- Income statement
- Will
- Trust

- Medications taken by your family member with special needs
- Therapy schedule (if your family member with special needs has one)
- Names and phone number of primary physician and specialists

The most important function of the binder or folder is to enable someone to help your family in an emergency by knowing where to turn for financial, medical, and legal help. With such a file, your family member will be better protected in an emergency. In a case of emergency, someone else will need to be able to step in to access your accounts, pay your bills, and find your legal documents. You want this person to spend time taking care of your family member with special needs, not spending days and weeks searching through jumbled paperwork.

Ideally, you will update this binder or folder with statements as you receive them. Some choose to update this information once or twice a year. Even if you forget, the binder or folder provides a helpful tool for someone else. Having these documents in one place, even if they are a year old, provides a valuable map in case of emergency. This Building Block adds a basic level of organization to your financial life.

GET READY TO BUILD

Thinking and planning before you build leads to better results than if you just have a collection of building materials, a few ideas, and jump in. My children went to a cooperative preschool where students were encouraged to hammer, saw, and build using wood, fabric, glue, and nails. The creations were amazing—but the real joy was in the playing and building, not in the end result. It was hard to see what the four-years-olds were trying to build. Most of them were just having fun without any end in mind.

Blueprints is different. It guides you to positive results for your family. It provides the basis for the life you want and ensures a high quality of life for your family members. It puts your financial and legal life to work to care for your family. The results matter for your family—you want the best for each of your family members, and it is time to take the steps to get there.

BUILDING BLOCK 4

The Special-Needs Trust

BUILDING YOUR FOUNDATION

Ahouse needs to rest on a strong foundation. Without it, the house crumbles.

The foundation for Blueprints planning is the special-needs trust. Without that trust, your financial planning crumbles.

The special-needs trust is intended to protect government benefits and provide assets to fund a high quality of life for your family member with a disability.

There are two crucial government programs available to help support your family member with special needs: Supplemental Security Income and Medicaid-funded comprehensive services. Those government benefits are worth a lot of money, and proper planning allows you to leave money for your family member with special needs without making mistakes that prevent her from getting SSI and comp services through Medicaid.

Supplemental Security Income (SSI) provides income support to your family member with special needs at age eighteen. In Colorado and most other states, this income benefit paid $735 per month in 2017.

Individuals receiving SSI also gain access to Medicaid, which covers health care and Medicaid-funded comprehensive services (comp services). In most states, the best nonprofits supporting people with special needs are funded through Medicaid.

A person with special needs can receive SSI and Medicaid benefits starting at age eighteen after the Social Security Administration verifies that she has a qualifying disability. Be aware that a resource test must be passed before anyone can gain access to SSI. "Resource" means assets. A person with special needs does not get SSI if she has more than $2,000 in disallowed resources (assets) in her name. This is why proper planning on your part is so important.

You can make mistakes in your finances and get it to work out over time. You can delay investing for six months or a year and make up for lost time down the road. You can choose a bad investment as part of a portfolio, pay off debts more slowly than desired, or buy a car that may be a bit too expensive—and you can recover from all of those things easily enough. But the quality of life for your family member with special needs will suffer if do not take care of the foundation. He may have years of lousy care and a poor lifestyle if there are no benefits available. He may lose the ability to have vacations, decent furnishings, and access to entertainment if you do not get your trust in place.

THE NUMBERS ARE BIG

Take a look at these numbers:

$263,880
$1,200,000

Now look at them again: Two hundred sixty-three thousand and eight hundred and eighty dollars. One million two hundred thousand dollars.

Those are some pretty serious numbers.

SSI pays people with special needs monthly income. In 2016, each individual who qualified for SSI received the monthly benefit payment of $733. That means that over thirty years, a person on SSI will receive $263,880 in monthly payments. That's a whole lot of money.

Comprehensive Medicaid-funded services—like living in a group home, supported working arrangements, and medical costs—can cost $40,000 or more per year. Over a period of thirty years, this benefit is worth $1,200,000 to a person with special needs.

This is real money used to support your family member.

This is real money that is lost if you do not put the foundation of a special-needs trust in place.

Ask yourself what steps you would take to get more than a million dollars. Would you get up every day at 5 a.m. for a week, a month, or a year? Would you walk five miles across town to pick up the check? Would you meet with a key professional for a few hours? What steps would you take to gain a million dollars?

How much would you spend to make sure this money was secured—$100, $1,000, $5,000, $10,000? All these amounts seem small compared to securing more than $1,000,000.

Oddly, the answer seems to be that most people will not take the simple steps to pick up the phone and spend a small amount of money to gain and protect what could amount to more than $1,000,000 for their family member with special needs. It seems unbelievable that right now there is a guaranteed way to have monthly income, health care, and service support, yet many families choose to do nothing to ensure it is available.

Every time I speak to groups of families with members who have special needs, I ask the same two questions.

The first: "How many of you have heard of special-needs trusts?" In most cases, more than half of the audience has heard of special-needs trusts and has some idea of why they need one.

The second: "How many of you have a special-needs trust?" Only about 15 percent of people in the groups have been to a lawyer and put a special-needs trust in place.

That percentage is low. Shockingly low.

A special-needs trust is a planning tool that helps protect government benefits for your family member with special needs. With a special-needs trust, you can keep assets in your family instead of spending them to replace the safety net provided by Medicaid and Supplemental Security Income.

Putting a special-needs trust in place for your family is Building Block 4 of the Blueprints process.

This Building Block will walk you through the key terms and steps that prepare you to meet with a qualified attorney and put together your legal plan to protect your family. The process can be finished in a few meetings with a good lawyer. If you prepare properly, you can have your legal work done within thirty days.

Give yourself a deadline to meet with an attorney. Do not put this off. Get over your procrastination, fear, or whatever is stopping you from taking this step. You cannot move forward without having your foundation in place. This chapter will explain terms and decision points for you to think about before you even walk into a lawyer's office.

Right now, commit to a deadline and write it down here:

I will meet with an attorney to start discussing a special-needs trust before _____ (date).

Now, hold yourself to this deadline to move your Blueprints planning forward and reduce stress for yourself.

Reasons to Plan

The reasons to plan are simple.

You can protect hundreds of thousands of dollars of benefits for your family member with special needs with just a few hours of meetings and a few thousand dollars.

You can avoid creating a disaster for a spouse, siblings, children, or anyone else who has to clean up the mess left behind when no estate plan is in place.

You can leave instructions for your family.

You choose the person best able to care for your family member with special needs.

Your estate plan gives trusted advisers the tools needed to help accomplish your goals.

Didn't commit?

Obviously, there are a number of solid reasons why you should plan. If you didn't make a commitment to get the process started, you have obstacles to overcome.

What stopped you?

UNDERSTAND YOUR FEARS

Why do so few families have a special-needs trust in place? It is not from a lack of information. We live in a world flooded with information. A quick internet search yields dozens of informative links about trusts and why they are needed.

Here's the real reason: People fail to act because of fear. They fear planning. They fear the future. They fear making a mistake.

Some people fear the legal world. The legal world seems complicated to most of us who are not lawyers. The words used by lawyers seem foreign. The court system appears unfriendly. We don't know whether the advice provided by a lawyer is good or bad because we are not familiar with the laws and language used when writing legal documents.

There are other obstacles when it comes to working with an attorney. Some people don't want to seem unintelligent. I have spoken with many people who have great abilities in their chosen professions who have not gone to lawyers because they do not even know the basic questions to ask. They do not want to appear uninformed or out of touch.

Some people fear asking questions and not understanding the answers. You need to ask your lawyer several important questions about the work he does. You need to understand which answers to give at what time, and this chapter will help with that.

Others fear being taken advantage of. It can be hard to tell which lawyers to use and what a fair price is. The range of charges can be wide for the same type of planning depending on the lawyer you choose. A person with significant experience will charge more than someone just starting out. Some add additional documents and trusts to the basic plan, and the charge covers this work.

Many families do not think they have enough money to justify setting up a trust. They think that trusts are for the wealthy, and they don't understand how trusts work for special-needs families.

The biggest fears are those of the future. You have taken a giant step toward conquering those fears in the first chapters. The process of dreaming about the future reduces stress for most people, and you should have put that fear behind you.

Finally, others don't want to make a mistake. So they make the biggest mistake of all: they do nothing.

STEPPING PAST FEAR

The first Building Blocks get you moving past fear and indecision. The hardest part for most families is to actually sit in one place, think about the future, and write down their goals. But now you've done that, so you are ready and able to act. You have a DreamList to guide you, have decided on which goals are most important, and understand your current resources.

The foundation of the rest of your planning is the special-needs trust, and you can have it in place within thirty days.

There is no other financial planning technique where the impact is so clear. Take a step back and think about your own life. Where can you get something worth hundreds of thousands of dollars with just a few hours of time and a small financial investment? This is not late-night TV advertising where you must take this special offer today. This is a real-world, proven planning tool that has been a sanctioned technique since the passage of federal legislation in 1993.

This Building Block shows how you can create huge resources for your family in just a few hours and with just a few thousand dollars. It also gives you the language to know and the outcomes you should expect. Armed with these things, you can move past any fears you may have about meeting with a lawyer to put your estate plan in place.

Let's look at the main obstacles that keep families from establishing an estate plan.

LACK OF UNDERSTANDING

The first obstacle is the lack of information about special-needs trusts—how they work and why they are important. You may not be sure of what the special-needs trust does and why you need one.

A special-needs trust can protect thousands, tens of thousands, and hundreds of thousands of dollars of public benefits. These trusts are allowed by Congress for people with developmental disabilities to preserve and build a quality of life better than that provided under public benefit programs.

The key federal programs for people with developmental disabilities are Supplemental Security Income (SSI) and Medicaid. These were created during the Johnson administration to improve the quality of life for people with developmental disabilities (and others) who could not find work, did not have access to medical benefits, and were deemed in need of a safety net. These programs were not designed to make a person rich or pay for the type of life most of us prefer to live. These programs were designed to provide food, shelter, and medical benefits.

To receive benefits from the Supplemental Security Income program, a person must have a qualifying disability. The list and types of disabilities are on the Social Security website, and there is a process through which the Social Security Administration makes a medical determination of the disability. Some—such as people with Down syndrome—qualify fairly easily. Others must present more details and case histories of their disabilities to become eligible. People who don't qualify when they first apply may find their condition changes, and they may gain access to programs later in life.

The person with a qualifying disability must also meet a resource test in which the government looks at that person's assets. A person with more than $2,000 in countable resources will not qualify, even if disabled. So what counts as a "resource" for SSI? This includes investment accounts, bank accounts, land, commodities, and most other assets a person with special needs may have. Certain assets do not count and are excluded from the calculation. A person with special needs can own a home, a vehicle, personal household items, and a small funeral policy. A properly drafted and funded special-needs trust does not count as a resource in the eyes of the Social Security Administration.

There is also an income test for receiving any or all of the SSI benefit and maintaining access to Medicaid. The amount varies by state. You will need a special-needs trust unless you expect your family member to have a full work history and to earn enough to live a comfortable lifestyle for his whole life. I do not know at this time if my minor daughter will have the ability or opportunity to work enough to live comfortably, so I have a special-needs trust in place.

A special-needs trust holds resources—bank accounts, invest-ment accounts, artwork, land, real estate, and any other assets—for the benefit of the person with special needs. This type of trust allows for money to be used and spent for the person with a disability and keeps the person covered by SSI and Medicaid. SSI benefits provide some basics for a person to live—generally, payments are made for food, shelter, and a small amount of personal needs. On the other hand, the trust assets can be used for vacations, subscriptions, work supports, entertainment, and so much more. The trust gives your family member a chance to live with dignity and joy.

Do not let your lack of understanding of all the details of special-needs trusts get in your way of not finding the right financial team and attorney to put a trust in place.

LACK OF MONEY

Some of you may wonder where to find a few thousand dollars for legal fees. You may even wonder where you will find a few hundred dollars in an emergency. Blueprints will help you stay focused on building your financial health. You need to get out of debt, build an emergency fund, and save for future expenses. You need to find a way to pay for a special-needs trust to protect your son or daughter as soon as possible.

The need for a trust is so important that I hope it acts as a key motivator for you in changing your current financial life. Do not let debt rule your life anymore. Build a strong financial platform. Let your family member with a disability be the main reason to get moving in the right direction.

Look around for the money to pay for a trust. Do you have a family member who can pay for the legal work? My local Down syndrome association provides a legal benefit through their scholarship program. It does not pay enough to get all the legal work done, but it does cut the out-of-pocket expense. Check with your local bar association to see if they have attorneys who donate their time. Look to see if you can cut back on other spending for a short time to get this work finished.

Remember the numbers from earlier in the chapter. Spending a few thousand dollars to get your legal work done can lead to tens of thousands or hundreds of thousands of dollars of benefit in the future. This is a great investment.

IT'S COMPLICATED

Special-needs trusts, wills, beneficiaries, guardians—the whole process and all the terms seem complicated—and people tend to avoid the complicated.

Special-needs planning looks complicated only because you have not done it before. There are new words to learn, new people to meet, and new decisions to make. Luckily, the people you hire will have experience putting together trusts and wills. You do not need to know every last detail about a special-needs trusts. You need to hire the most qualified person in your community to help you understand your goals and to draft the documents. Let your financial planner and attorney make it less complicated, and move ahead.

UNCERTAINTY ABOUT BENEFITS

The news keeps us scared and worried about the future of benefits. On any given day, we can read, watch, or listen to someone telling us the government is running out of money, Social Security is bankrupt, and Medicaid will be cut. The headlines have not changed much since my daughter was born thirteen years ago, and I bet they have been fairly steady since the introduction of Medicaid programs in the 1960s.

So far, I have not seen much change in the attitude that public benefits programs should continue to help those who cannot help themselves. People with qualifying disabilities did not choose their disability—they were born with autism or Down syndrome, got into a car accident, or became disabled through some series of events outside their control. Social Security and Medicaid are safety nets that provide the most basic needs of human existence. They do not enrich the people who are served.

Of course, these benefits could change down the road. But it is also true that the trust in place for my daughter will be a helpful and important planning tool even if benefits are reduced or cut. I need to plan today with the knowledge I have today. The benefit programs of the last fifty years will not disappear overnight, and I recommend planning with that in mind.

TOO LITTLE TIME

For many, the thought of finding an attorney and sitting down to put together the estate plan seems like it will take forever. It does not. You can put your trust in place and be started in the right direction in just a few hours. You can take a few steps in a short time to make a huge change in the future.

In the first section of this book, you have helped yourself carve out time to think about special-needs planning. At this point you should understand the value of a few hours of time and some dollars spent. The issue for most families is not really one of time—it is getting excited and passionate about making the change. Time works for you when you take action today.

FINDING THE RIGHT LAWYER

You will build a team of professionals to help you along the way. You may have never worked with a financial planner, lawyer, or CPA, and you may be worried about choosing the right ones. The good thing is that once you find one good professional, that person can help you find the other team members. This Building Block will help you know which questions to ask lawyers to discover whether they have the experience and knowledge needed to help you.

MAKING A PERMANENT MISTAKE

There are few mistakes in special-needs planning that cannot be corrected. You have to look at mistakes as learning opportunities and use them to improve how you save, invest, and make decisions.

Special-needs trusts have a word in them that increases fear: *irrevocable. Irrevocable* sounds bad—it means I cannot take something back that I have done. You cannot take money out of a contribution made to an irrevocable trust. You cannot change the trust language once it is set up and funded.

But even with these irrevocable trusts, you can likely recover from any mistakes you may make. Most of the time, special-needs trusts are not funded until someone passes away. This gives you lots of time to think about your decision after it is made and change your trust if needed. You can create a new trust if you made a huge mistake in your first one. Most people create a good trust the first time, so do not spend too much time thinking you will make a mistake. Use that time to think of all the positive outcomes you'll create by having a trust in place.

MOVING FORWARD AND TAKING ACTION

You are ready. You understand the purpose of a special-needs trust—to hold money and other assets for your family member with special needs and to help that person qualify for government benefits, like Supplemental Security Income and Medicaid. You have thought about what's holding you back, and you have realized your fears are like those annoying summer gnats in your backyard. Swat them away. They are small and can be handled.

The next few steps should be fairly simple if you do them in the right order.

Take the following steps to prepare yourself to go to your attorney, and you will make the process easier and quicker for everyone involved.

The first meeting with a lawyer is when you review your financial situation, discuss the goals of your estate plan, and let the lawyer know the key people involved in your planning. Who will get your stuff? What will happen to your minor children? How will assets be distributed? Who steps in to help with financial issues? Who can make medical decisions for you?

The lawyer will write the documents for you. Your main job is to be prepared to identify the people involved in your estate plan and what assets and liabilities you have. Bring your balance sheet and income statement with you to the first meeting. Take the worksheets from this section, as they will help the lawyer know what to do with your estate.

KNOW AND CHOOSE THE PEOPLE INVOLVED IN THE TRUST

Write down the key people you'll name in your legal documents. By the end of this part of the chapter, you will have put names in place for your trustee and guardian, decided how to split your assets, and made other significant decisions to help you get your special-needs trust and estate plan in place.

Beneficiaries

A beneficiary is the person (or organization) who gets your money and other assets when you die—the one who benefits from the money you leave in your will or trust.

You choose where this goes. You can leave everything to one person or split it many ways. You can give one person half of your money and split the rest however you want. It is completely up to you.

Spouses usually give each other everything they own, but that's not mandatory. Many states require that spouses receive some amount of inheritance so the surviving spouse is not impoverished if all the assets transfer to children.

Children are usually the next in line to receive money from parents. Your estate plan takes the part for your family member with special needs and funds the special-needs trust. Other children may receive theirs in trust as well if they are minors or until they reach a certain age, or you can give them their share outright.

You can also choose other people to receive money—a friend, nephew, niece, or anyone else.

You can also choose nonprofit organizations to receive some of your assets.

You get to choose.

You will likely have one or more *primary beneficiaries* and one or more *contingent beneficiaries.* Primary beneficiaries are the first people in line. Contingent beneficiaries are the people who get the assets if the primary is no longer alive. Your spouse or partner is likely your primary beneficiary. Your children are likely your contingent beneficiaries. At this stage, do not separate out your family member with special needs in any way. Include that person on your list. The portion for that family member will go to a trust.

You may have children from more than one marriage, grandchildren, nieces, nephews, or friends you wish to include. List as many as you wish. You should also put down any charities, religious organizations, or foundations here.

Remember, the goal of this book is to take the subjects you have been avoiding or did not know what to do with and turn the process into a series of simple steps. The next few exercises will help you identify the people you want to receive your estate.

 Worksheet: Key People—Beneficiaries

Start with your primary beneficiary. Is there one person or a group of people who will split your estate when you pass away?

Write down the names of the people you wish to receive a portion of your estate.

You can choose to leave all your assets to one person or split them into as many parts as you want.

Many of my clients are married with children. They list their spouse as the primary beneficiary for everything.

One of my clients is close to ninety years old. Her husband is no longer alive, and she lists her many children as primary beneficiaries, with equal shares going to each child. Some of my clients are divorced and married again. Sometimes these families leave money to their children and their current spouses.

You may want to leave 100 percent to your spouse (see example #1). If that is the case, write your spouse's name on line 1, specify 100 percent, and skip to the next section. You may not have a spouse, or you may have other reasons to leave less than 100 percent to your spouse (see example #2). If this is the case, write the other names and percentages as well.

1.	%
2.	%
3.	%
4.	%
5.	%

Example #1

1. Kelly	100%

Example #2

1. Kelly	70%
2. Benjamin	10%
3. Sarah	10%
4. Anna	10%

Contingent Beneficiaries

The next section lists your most important contingent beneficiaries. These are the people who receive your assets if your spouse or partner (or other first beneficiary) is no longer alive. For families with children with special needs, the primary beneficiary is usually the spouse, and the contingent beneficiaries the children (using a trust for the person with special needs).

How Much for Your Family Member with Special Needs?

The biggest question families have is how much to leave to each child. Should you leave more, the same, or less to your family member with special needs?

There is no right answer. Some people look at government benefits and say the person with a disability needs less money than their other children, as the person receiving SSI and Medicaid-funded services will have their basic needs already met. Others say the opposite—they expect typical family members to work and pay for the costs of their own lives, so they leave most to the special-needs trust. Others split things equally.

As I write this, my estate plan shows an equal split. My children are young, and I have no idea what their capabilities as working adults will be. I expect the best from all of my children and hope they will not need any of the money I plan to leave to them. The portion of my will that tells how much goes to each child or trust can be changed later. My expectation is that I will change the percentages at some point down the road once I have a better idea of where my children are in life. You can do the same. Make a determination today, and understand that you can change this later if you need to.

List your contingent beneficiaries and percentages here.

1.	%
2.	%
3.	%
4.	%
5.	%

 Worksheet: Key People—Contingent Beneficiaries

Do not leave your estate plan a mystery. You do not need to have a dramatic reading of the will by the personal representative in an attorney's office. Your personal representative does not need a lawsuit against the estate that he has to handle because you have not told your family members that they will be receiving an inheritance. Remember that you need to find a way to let those you leave out of the will or trust know that they are not getting anything, especially if they think they are getting part of your estate.

PERSONAL REPRESENTATIVE

Your personal representative (sometimes referred to as an executor) takes over when you pass away. This representative distributes your money to your heirs and sets up trusts. This person also steps in to handle many aspects of your financial life—for example, she might sign the contract to sell your house, file taxes, pay bills, and more.

You want to choose someone you like and trust to fill this job. She will have to have the ability to handle money, read credit card and investment statements, and organize your assets. Your personal representative will be the person who hires an attorney to review your will, file court documents, finalize your estate, hire an accountant to submit tax returns, and work with the financial planner to distribute investment assets.

Choose a person who has the life experience and is responsible enough to handle your estate. This can be an easy task if you have a simple estate and you won't need a personal representative with extensive experience in investments, tax, or law. If your estate is complicated, you own a business, you have rental properties, or you own interests in trusts or other more complex assets, then designate a person with the right experience.

Write down three people who can act as your personal representative. Your attorney will help you choose one after asking you about the specific reasons for your choices.

1.

2.

3.

 Worksheet: Key People—Personal Representative

TRUSTEE

Another key person to name in your will is a trustee.

The personal representative's job is limited. He handles assets, but only to distribute them to the right people, trusts, or other heirs following a death. He reads the will and follows your instructions to make sure everything is handled according to your wishes.

The trustee steps in after the personal representative finishes the job of transferring money to heirs and trusts. The money left for your family member will go to a trust to be spent on him, and the trustee will be the person in charge of that trust.

The trust becomes the "legal owner" of any assets in it, such as investment accounts, real estate, or CDs. A trust is like a person with an odd name. Instead of *Rob Wrubel* owning everything, everything is now owned by something called *The Special-Needs Trust to Benefit Rob Wrubel*. This name will appear on bank records, deeds, titles, investment accounts, stock certificates, and anywhere else the name of the owner of the trust assets appears.

The trustee's job continues as long as assets remain in the trust. It is a long-term commitment to help the beneficiary of a trust. The trustee will handle assets, pay bills, send out money, and report taxes for the life of the trust, which could last decades.

The trustee is the person who is allowed to buy and sell assets, pay debts and expenses, or make any changes of assets inside the trust. In a special-needs trust, the trustee acts without asking permission from anyone else. The only thought of the trustee when making any decision should be, "Is this in the best interests of the person with special needs who is the beneficiary of the trust?" The trustee must act for the benefit of the person for whom the money is to be used.

You can choose a family member or friend to be trustee, or someone who would be considered a "personal" trustee. The trend these days is for people to name a personal trustee. You will want to choose a person who makes good decisions; can handle money; knows how to work with financial planners, accountants, and attorneys; and knows your family member with special needs.

The other option is to choose a "corporate" trustee. These trustees are investment firms, banks, or trust companies that handle the day-to-day work of trust administration. Some people prefer a corporate trustee if they do not personally know anyone who is able or responsible enough to act as a trustee.

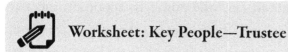

Worksheet: Key People—Trustee

Write down the names of three potential personal trustees.

1.

2.

3.

Successor Trustee

During a lifetime, people move from state to state or country to country. Managing a trust from a different state is not too difficult. Managing a trust from the other side of the world is nearly impossible.

You named your top pick to the position of trustee. The next two should be named as successor trustees. The successor trustee steps in and becomes trustee if the first person you picked cannot or does not want to stay on as trustee.

Also, write your trust giving your trustee the ability to resign at any point. Special-needs trusts can be around for decades, and people move, marry, or have their lives change in unpredictable ways. There may come a point when your personal trustee is not capable of continuing to act in that capacity.

Money could be in this trust a long time, especially if it gets funded with a parent's early death or by grandparents when they pass away. The first trustee may choose to resign as he ages, moves out of the area, or needs to focus on other major life events.

I prefer trusts where the trustee can choose her own replacement. You are picking the person you think best able to make decisions for your family member. Trustees are authorized to spend money on medical care, vacations, clothing, and entertainment. They hire people to invest money, prepare the tax return, and handle any legal issues. This person should have the power to appoint a successor when the time comes as well. This power lets the current trustee use your successor list as a starting point for finding the right person and also gives them some flexibility in making the best choice.

CONTINGENT BENEFICIARIES OF THE SPECIAL-NEEDS TRUST

The entire purpose of the special-needs trust is to improve the life of a person with a disability. This person is the primary beneficiary of the trust. The money and assets in the trust are to be used to benefit this person. The trustee cannot use this money for his own benefit or for that of anyone else. The money spent must support the person with special needs.

If the person with special needs passes away and there is still something left in the trust, who gets the money? You will write in your trust the names of the people, religious institutions, or charities you wish to receive the remaining amounts in the trust. You can split this however you want—for example, to siblings, to your church, or to the supporting nonprofit agencies that cared for your daughter—in whatever amounts you wish. These are called the contingent beneficiaries, and they get assets that remain if not used to support the person with special needs.

GUARDIAN

What happens to your young children or family member should you die? Who will take care of your family when you are not there to do it? If your children are all under the age of eighteen, you will designate a family member or close personal friend to take your children into their home. When you die, your minor children move to the new home. The person you appoint as guardian could live a block away or on the other side of the country. No matter what, your children move to that home. You do not want the court to decide who will care for your children, so make sure you choose someone as guardian and name that person in your will.

Designate a guardian in your legal plans. The guardian takes care of the health and well-being of the person with special needs (while the trustee takes care of the money. The guardian is the person who steps in as replacement for Mom or Dad in raising young children and making sure an adult person with special needs is in a safe living environment.

Your adult family member with special needs may not need a guardian—but if he does, the guardian may find a host home, service agency, or other organization to provide needed living support. As with a trustee, the guardian can be an individual or an organization.

You will need to speak with the person or people you choose before writing them into your will. Do not assume that the person you choose wants to step in as guardian. This is a more difficult, time-consuming, and emotionally engaging role than that of trustee. Your minor children will live with the guardian. Your adult family member with special needs will need a guardian who can speak with provider agencies, make trips from time to time to check on your adult family member, and handle other decisions about daily living. The guardian should be both loving and capable of communicating with others, as she will be the key person between your family member and the world.

Write down three people who could act as guardian. Your attorney will help you choose one after asking you about the specific reasons for your choices.

 Worksheet: Key People—Guardian

1.

2.

3.

SHOULD THE TRUSTEE AND GUARDIAN BE THE SAME PERSON?

You have several lists from this chapter. One list has people you will name for legal and financial issues. The other list has names of people who will work with personal and life issues. Do your lists have the same people on both? Are they different?

The roles and responsibilities of the trustee and guardian look and feel very different. The trustee handles money, taxes, and legal issues. The trustee makes payments to improve the life of the beneficiary. The guardian works with people and organizations on issues of daily living—homes, social life, work, community, and health. The guardian seeks to make each day the best it can be.

These two areas intersect as money from the trust is used to support a person's life. The people involved in those roles may come to their job with different attitudes and skill sets. To get a good picture of this, think about the difference in stereotypes between a second-grade teacher and a banker.

The Second-Grade Teacher

Think about the people you meet who teach second grade. What comes to mind? Kind people. Caring people. Helpful, nurturing people. Teachers spend time on the floor or sitting in small chairs with a hand on the shoulder of a student. They urge their students to read, behave well, and learn the simple pleasures of life. Second-grade teachers smile a lot during the day. They are warm, caring, and involved in every aspect of the students' lives every day of the school year. This is the type of person I want as guardian of my children and someone one who can work with my daughter when she is an adult and I am no longer alive. I want someone who's loving, patient, and willing to take the time needed to make life the best it can be for my daughter.

The Banker

Now think about your image of a banker. What comes to mind? Numbers. Spreadsheets. Procedures. Bankers make quick decisions involving numbers and money without spending too much time with people. Bankers look to the future; they need to think about the economy, cash flow, and business when helping clients raise funds or improve their businesses. They seek to understand the facts in the analysis of their decisions. This is the type of person you may want for a trustee.

So, can one person fill both roles? Your family member needs a person who can think like a banker and act like a second-grade teacher. Can anyone on your list handle both? Usually the answer is no. Some people are more wired for facts, while others are more in touch with feelings. Some are more like a banker, while others are more like a second-grade teacher.

There are other reasons to separate these jobs. A trustee and guardian working together over time make better decisions. They work with each other, rely on each other, and use each other to review any issues that may come up. Separating the guardian and trustee jobs allows those two people to talk to each other and reduces the pressure on one person to make every decision alone.

The two together can create a plan with their financial planner to determine the best use of funds over the appropriate time period. Second-grade teacher types acting as trustee tend to spend too quickly. Banker types sometimes hold money for too long.

In my work with families, I see money spent quickly when the guardian also acts as trustee.

Recently, a trustee called to ask for more money from a trust we manage. This trustee has the second-grade teacher heart. She wants the best for the person she helps. Unfortunately, this person calls each month for more money, and in fewer than two years has spent more than two-thirds of the money in the trust. Each time she calls, she tells us she will not be calling again anytime soon and that this should be the last withdrawal for a long time. We know the money is being spent to support the person with special needs and to make his life better today. We also know that before long, there will not be any money left and that the person with special needs will still need money for clothing, vacations, and household goods for years to come. This trustee/guardian would have been better off resigning and letting someone with a banker's mindset create a more sensible spending plan.

So often guardians wish to make life for the person with special needs better today and will use as much money as possible to meet that goal. But special-needs trust money often needs to last for decades. This tension between spending today and saving and investing for the future never goes away in the trust. Trustees with a banker mentality do a better job in preserving money for future years while still taking care of present needs.

WHAT DOES THE TRUSTEE DO?

Simply put, the trustee makes payments to improve the life of your family member with special needs. Some of the trustee's duties are required by law. She must manage money and other assets in the trust for the beneficiary. She must file a tax return for the trust. She must not use the trust to benefit herself and is to use the trust to improve the life of the person with special needs. The trustee can hire any and all professionals and people as needed to perform these duties.

You can write your trust with broad and open directions to the trustee. Basically, you tell the trustee to do what she thinks best. You do not have to say much more than this, and limiting it to this gives your trustee as much flexibility as possible. Remember, life changes, and you want your trustee to be able to adapt as needed.

If you would rather, you can direct the trustee or provide tips for the trustee in your trust. The trust is one place where you can make decisions on behalf of your family member after you have passed away. You can suggest or require the trustee to pay for certain items if you wish, but the trust cannot be written to make specific payments at specific times—these must be decided on and made by the trustee.

The trust can be written with as many or as few special provisions as you desire. One family I spoke with wanted to make sure the son would be able to wear trendy clothes. The clothing budget was not specified, but the desire to have nice-looking, fashionable clothing was. That was as important to this family as going to the movies and taking trips were for other families.

Does it make sense to put specific spending ideas or investment restrictions in your trust? Most of the time it does not. You want your trust to be open and flexible. Think about the pace of change we see around us today. A trust funded thirty years ago could not have predicted the wide use of the internet, iPhones, iPads, and other digital devices. A trust written thirty years ago could have spelled out that the trust would be used to purchase vinyl albums and record players. Today, a trustee would have a hard time finding records—or even a record store. The world changes, and your trust must be able to adapt.

Your family member with special needs will change too. My children are young, and I cannot imagine what they will be like in ten, twenty, or fifty years. Their interests will change. Their needs will change. Their social lives, living situations, and eating habits will likely be different. The trust cannot possibly know what will be needed in the future. You have to rely on a trustee to be able to make decisions to keep pace.

MANAGE ASSETS

The trust will have certain assets it owns. It will have a bank account. It will have an investment account. It may own real estate, such as a house or land. The trust can own just about anything you can own unless you tell it not to. Trusts can own businesses, jewelry, artwork, cars, and more.

The trustee decides what the trust owns unless you have given the trustee restrictions or mandates.

The trustee does not have to manage the assets on his own and usually does not. Trustees hire financial advisers, real-estate agents, business managers, and professionals as needed.

Before committing money to investments, the trustee should adopt a plan for the trust that is based on the current and future needs of the person with special needs who benefits from the trust. Ideally, the trustee works with the person with special needs (to the extent possible), the guardian, and any other key people to sketch out the plan.

Some people with special needs have significant medical issues that impact life expectancy. In this case, the money in the trust will be spent more quickly to make the most of a short amount of time. This money will also be invested more conservatively, as it will be needed sooner.

Others have long life expectancies, and the money in the trust may be needed over decades. The trustee may decide to look for ways to create income from the trust that can be spent while trying to grow the assets over time. The trustee may also need to keep certain amounts in cash for emergency medical or housing issues.

No matter what the scenario, the trustee must invest and spend with the beneficiary in mind.

LEGAL AND TAX CONSIDERATIONS

The trustee's responsibilities include filing taxes each year with the IRS. Special-needs trusts pay taxes just like people do. Once a trust is funded, it will need to get a tax ID number and file a tax return each year. The trustee should hire an accountant with experience in trust tax accounting.

The trustee must keep on top of legal issues impacting the trust and the beneficiary. Medicaid and Social Security rules change, and these rule changes could impact the quality of life and benefit programs of the beneficiary. A good trustee regularly reviews the trust document as it relates to benefit program changes, generally with the help of an attorney.

MAKE PAYMENTS

A key job of the trustee is to spend the money in the trust. The trustee gets to decide when money comes out of the trust and what it will be used for. No one else can do this. The beneficiary cannot use the trust like a checking account or credit card. The guardian cannot spend the money. A friend or work buddy cannot get at it. The trust document and the trustee make the final decision on how to use the money and when.

Usually, the trustee works with the guardian to understand how to spend the money. The guardian knows the needs and desires of the person with special needs. The trustee could also get input on how to spend assets from the team involved in making life best for the person. This can include input from caregivers, medical professionals, employers, teachers, and friends.

Medicaid rules mean that the trustee cannot spend the money on certain items or in certain ways. Right now, the list of allowable spending is much longer than the list of spending that is disallowed. Money from the trust cannot be used to replace or add to benefits provided by government programs. Basically, this means trust funds cannot be used for food or rent. Government benefits pay for a roof over someone's head and for food on the table. Without a trust, your family member with special needs has a place to live and food to eat. With a trust, individuals with a disability can have the other aspects of life you wish them to have, and their lives can be similar to the one you're providing them today.

Sometimes it is hard to believe that a person can live well on the amount paid by the government programs. The monthly SSI payment is not a reasonable amount for housing, food, and other living expenses combined. People without trusts are limited in the quality of life they have. Most people with developmental disabilities live with additional housing benefits provided under other programs, like Section 8, to be able to find a reasonable apartment. Most of the SSI benefit for people living under comp services goes to the service provider. The person served keeps just a small amount for personal needs.

The trust, on the other hand, gives color and joy to life. It helps support a person in living a full and well-rounded life. Some examples of what the trust can pay for include:

- Furniture
- TVs
- Stereos
- Cable or satellite
- Newspaper and magazine subscriptions
- Curtains

- Fish tanks
- Therapies not covered by Medicaid
- Vacations
- Phones

A trust can pay for a long list of items—shoes, sports equipment, movie tickets and popcorn, therapies, and just about anything not included under food and rent.

A special-needs trust cannot pay rent or add to the rent portion of living expenses to improve a person's living situation. One way around this is for them to own the apartment or home where the beneficiary lives. Many like this option as it provides the chance to choose where the person will live with less risk in having to move down the road.

The trustee must be careful in making payments out of the trust. The money cannot go to the beneficiary directly. The person with special needs cannot be given cash or anything that can be turned into cash (like certain gift cards). Money must be spent for the sole benefit of the beneficiary. It cannot go to other individuals unless certain circumstances are met.

So how do payments get made? The trustee can use a debit card, checks, credit cards, or online payments. Any purchases must be made directly to the provider or retailer. Trips to Disneyland are popular expenditures from trusts. The trustee can work with a travel agent and pay the agent directly for the plane and hotel. Travel groups that take people with disabilities on trips near and far have sprung up all around the country.

FIND THE RIGHT LAWYER

Special-needs trusts constitute a unique area of estate planning. You want to find an attorney who has experience working with families like yours in your state. I have seen trusts written by attorneys where the trust does not meet the standards of qualification in my state. I have seen trusts where the wrong beneficiary name was used or the trustee's name was incorrect.

Start by asking your CPA, financial planner, real-estate agent, or homeowner's insurance agent for the names of attorneys they recommend. You will soon find the names of attorneys who work fairly, honestly, and competently with families who have a member with special needs. Your local bar association will also have the names of attorneys. Make sure you ask the person you speak to for someone who has experience in working on special-needs trusts.

Interview the attorney before committing to work with her. Most will give you an hour or so of consultation before you have to spend any money. During that initial meeting, ask these key questions:

1. How many special-needs trusts have you drawn up this year or over the past several years? If the answer is one or two, you will want to find a different attorney. Most attorneys will not remember the exact number. You want to listen to see if this is something an attorney does regularly or only from time to time.

2. Do you take continuing education classes on special-needs planning? Lawyers must take many hours of ongoing education to keep their licenses current. They have a choice of what types of classes to take on different parts of law. You want your lawyer to stay up to date on issues and changes that impact special-needs trusts.

3. How do you charge? Most lawyers in estate planning charge a flat fee, depending on the project. You need to know before you start what to expect. As you interview lawyers, you may hear that some charge more or less. Ask why they charge what they charge. Is the work the same from one attorney to another? Is the quality the same? You will get an idea of what

the average costs in your area are if you speak with several attorneys. You should expect to pay more than your friends without special-needs family members, as they do not have the complex issue of special-needs trusts in their lives.

Over the next few weeks, you will have your legal work finished. The hardest part of finishing the special-needs trust is getting the right people in place—and you have just completed the exercises that helped you name those people. Your lawyer will put together the language of the trust, but she cannot move forward until you have given her the names of the beneficiaries, trustee, guardian, and personal representative.

 Worksheet: Choosing an Attorney

COMMUNICATE THE PLAN

Unfortunately, your plan could still fail. You have taken the necessary steps to protect SSI and Medicaid by making sure your son or daughter does not have any countable resources. The amount of money you plan to give your child will go to the special-needs trust instead of being an asset of your child. But what if someone else in your family decides to leave money for your son or daughter and does not know the SSI and Medicaid rules? The next exercise will help you prevent other people from causing your family member with special needs to lose benefits.

One client of mine had a sister who wanted to do something for her niece with a disability. The aunt had a life-insurance policy and planned to name the niece as the beneficiary of the policy. More than $100,000 would go to the niece when the aunt passed away.

While that may seem generous, it posed a big problem.

The Social Security and Medicaid offices do not care where the money comes from. They care that the person with a qualifying disability has countable resources more than $2,000. My client's daughter would lose benefits at the time of her sister's death, as the money from the life-insurance policy would now be a countable resource. This mistake could be fixed, but it would be expensive, time-consuming, and stressful—and would likely leave a gap in benefits. This is a problem easily avoided.

Are there family members and friends who wish to do something good for you or your family member with special needs? If they want to provide gifts and support, welcome their help, but help them do that in a way that does not cause jeopardize the future security of your family member.

In the next worksheet, write down the names of people you need to talk to—and to whom you need to explain how your estate plan is designed to protect benefits for your family member with special needs. Help these people understand how the trust will provide a higher quality of life than what the regular benefits provide.

 Worksheet: Communicate Your Plans

Write down the names of people who need to know about your plan. These people may not have the ability or desire to give gifts to your family member with special needs, but they need to know about the work you have done. Write down the names of the people you need to talk to:

1. _____

2. _____

3. _____

4. _____

5. _____

Next, write down the names of the guardians and trustees you identified earlier.

Guardians:

1. _____

2. _____

3. _____

Trustees:

1. _____

2. _____

3. _____

Next, practice a short speech about your legal work and why you have done it. You are not asking for money or help—you are making sure everyone around you knows how important it is to talk to you about their plans if they decide to help. They do not need to know all the details of your estate plan. They do need to know that your plan is different from most plans and that they should talk to you before making any gifts of any kind to your family member with special needs. Make sure to speak with your guardian and trustee about choices as well, as they will need to know that there could be money available in the future.

Use this sample as a guide:

Mom and Dad [or insert name], we have taken steps to change our wills to protect [name of family member with special needs]. He can receive government benefits as a result of the steps we have taken. My planner/attorney recommended we speak to all family members and friends about this. [Name of person] cannot have any money. We will not leave anything to him when we pass away. We are talking to you to make sure you know how we are protecting those benefits. We do not know if you plan to include [name of person] in your will or as a beneficiary of any accounts. If you do, please let us know so we can give you the right information to protect [name of person]. Thank you for taking the time to listen.

The conversation about your planning goes best when you educate your family without asking for anything other than the time to listen. Remember, the only thing you can control is your estate plan. Ideally, the other family and friends who want to help will come to understand how important it is to get the planning right and coordinate their gifts with you.

BUILDING BLOCK 5

Eliminating Debt Forever

The United States Olympic Committee office building sits directly east of my office. When I look out my window, I see the rings and logo of the organization that helps American athletes train to compete across the globe. Six years ago, the building was a retail store selling Western clothing, and I had a great view of the project that converted the old building into a brand-new one.

The project seemed to take forever to finish. Construction and building projects seem to go on for months without anything ever happening. Initially there are people at the site with cameras, pickup trucks, and measuring instruments. At some point, the plows and bucket loaders come by—but still, there is nothing to say what the project will become. Then the foundation gets poured, and all of a sudden there's a frame, followed by walls, a roof, and windows.

The first four Building Blocks prepare you to do the work needed to build your dream home—a secure financial life where you can provide for each person in your household. You've done that preliminary work but have not yet improved your financial life. With this Building Block, that will happen.

You cannot build a strong financial foundation and security with debts on your balance sheet. Most Americans today live with their debts as with old friends—they have student loans for decades and credit card balances that never seem to go away. They bounce from one car loan to another while wondering why they have nothing in savings or in retirement funds.

The goal of Building Block 5 is to change your behavior and the way you think about debt, and to get rid of your debt forever. This chapter gives you basic tools for reducing and eliminating debt in your life so you can live a stress-free financial life and begin building wealth. You will focus on building savings, retirement funds, assets to fund a trust, and more after you have paid off your student loans, retired your credit card balances, and gotten rid of your car loans.

Are you willing to trade stress for peace? How about payments for investments? This Building Block takes energy, focus, patience, and determination. The rewards of your change in behavior today will come in the form of reduced stress, freedom to spend your earnings as you wish, and the ability to take care of yourself and your family member with special needs in the future.

Debt has more to do with human nature and behavior than the cost of making payments. It has to do with the desire to live debt-free and the passion to change spending patterns today to protect your family in the future.

Your debt will not disappear tomorrow. For most people it will take time—anywhere from a few months to a few years. The hole in your financial life may be big or small, but you will have to fill it in as you go along to build a strong financial foundation.

COMMITMENT

Eliminating debt forever requires a commitment today. You need to stop everything else you are doing, turn off the music, close your office door, and take a minute for yourself.

Now, say to yourself that you are committed to eliminating debt forever—that you are no longer a person who lives in debt, uses debt, or carries debt with you. You are a person free from debt who builds assets and income easily.

Find a way to say this in your own words. Write it down on a piece of paper, on a note card, or in your phone. At some point, you will be tempted to use your credit card, sign a car loan or lease, or borrow money. At these times, take out your note and repeat what you said—that you are committed to eliminating debt forever. Tape it to your credit card if you have to.

Use of debt is automatic for most people. We take out the credit card to pay for coffee, groceries, haircuts, and movie tickets. We do not think about the true cost of that credit card when we buy something. But that cost shows up later in the form of an 18-percent interest rate and, worse yet, in increasing stress.

Your commitment is not just to yourself. Your commitment is to your family. And families who have members with special needs have more goals than reducing stress and saving for retirement. Your commitments must include saving to provide a high quality of life for your family member with a disability. You cannot let your family members down by being financially irresponsible.

CREATING A NEW MINDSET

The biggest challenge is changing how you think about debt. You need a new mindset, a new way of looking at your financial world. You need to move from the mindset of a person with debt who uses debt and thinks debt is a usual part of a life to a person free from debt who is now in control of their financial life. Changing your mindset is key to building a solid financial life.

One person I knew earned a very good income, lived a reasonable lifestyle, and somehow still had tens of thousands of dollars of student loans fifteen years after leaving his professional training. He had an unreasonable attachment to the student loans and did not focus on getting rid of them. This client thought about the loans too much, worried about getting rid of them, and yet never focused his attention on actually getting rid of them. Building a family, working, and living got in the way. He found reasons to keep them. The interest rates were low. The family needed a ski cabin.

He did not save for retirement to the degree needed, in part because the loans were taking his extra income. His net worth did not grow, and it should have—his income could have supported his ability to save and invest.

The loans gave him the ability to pay for an education, and that education led to a career with high income. He could not have gotten there without the loans. He helps people every day in life and knows that his work is important.

Recently, he decided to pay off his loans. He cut back on certain living expenses, sold a second home (to eliminate the high mortgage payment), and focused on his student loans. The student loans were quickly put to rest once this happened, and my client realized he should have done this long ago. He still worries about money, but he does not have the same sense of fear he did when his liabilities were out of control. He now saves the maximum amount he can in his retirement account and has rebuilt an emergency fund. The financial stress of carrying around his student loans evaporated, and he wondered why he did not do it years before.

Here's why he didn't do it years earlier: he couldn't see a real reason for doing so. The dollar amount was manageable as long as he worked. The interest rates did not add up to much—it was "cheap" money. He figured the loans would just go away one day as long as he kept paying them down. Once he changed his mindset, he paid off the loans and opened the way for a new way of thinking and behaving. He went from a debtor mindset to a wealth mindset and has been making significant progress ever since.

Attitude. Commitment. Desire. Passion. Without these, you will not get out of debt. You will not change the way you accumulate assets. You will not have the resources you need to fund the life you dream of and to put money away to care for your family.

With the right attitude, commitment, desire, and passion, you can acquire the habits, strategies, and planning needed to achieve the financial stability you desire. How do you see yourself in one year? Out of debt, moving along to get out of debt, or in the same painful place you are today?

DETAILED BUILDING PLANS

You will need detailed plans to help you get out of debt and stay out of debt. These plans give you instructions each month on how to spend your money.

Think about the next stage of building a house. The foundation sits there, the concrete poured and ready for the rest of the house to go up on it. The framers do not just show up, take the wood sitting in a pile, and start putting pieces of wood on wood in a random order. They have detailed instructions from the architect and engineer telling them which pieces to use first, which types of wood go where, and what kind of supports and nails to use. The basic frame goes up following the design of the architect and homeowner.

The Building Block of getting out of debt starts with a detailed set of instructions about where your money goes before you ever have that money in your hands. Money will disappear as quickly as it comes if you do not tell it where to go. I know from experience.

For the longest time I have kept a $100 bill in my wallet. This is my last-minute cash—the money I use when I need cash and do not have my checkbook or cannot use my debit card. This situation happens less and less as just about everyone takes debit cards nowadays. Still, I like to have that $100 bill in my wallet.

Why do I keep a $100 bill and not five $20 bills? A funny thing happens when I have the $100. I almost never use it. That crisp $100 bill represents a lot of cash. I never like spending it on something small. Once the $100 is broken into smaller bills, the money just disappears, and I never know where it goes. Spending $5 here and $10 there just happens—a lunch, PTA dues, sports drinks for kids during soccer, and so on. The money flies out of the wallet once that $100 is broken.

The same thing happens with the money that comes into your house—your income—if you do not have a spending plan.

Your plan to spend money goes by a name—it's called a *budget*. A budget acts as your plan for your money before you ever get it. The budget lets you and your spouse or partner make decisions about how to spend, save, and invest your money over time. Your budget gives you control over your financial life rather than having your spending habits and debts control you.

FIRST STEPS

You need to get a clear understanding of how much money you earn and how much you spend each month. Start with a blank piece of paper or use the income worksheet.

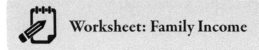 **Worksheet: Family Income**

Write down the amount you earn each month—your take-home pay after taxes and other deductions. Write down any income you get if you own rental properties or do side jobs.

 Worksheet: Family Expenses

Next, write down your categories of spending. These are rent or mortgage, health insurance, food, entertainment, dining out, therapy, and more. Do this quickly, and you should have most of your categories in place without too much effort.

The following is a list of sample categories:

- Mortgage (or rent)
- Utilities (gas, electric, water)
- Home/car insurance
- Health insurance (amount not deducted by employer)
- Life insurance
- Phone service (cell, home, internet)
- Cable/satellite
- Groceries
- Dining out
- Entertainment
- Therapies (music, occupational, or any other)
- Education (current expenses)
- Taxes owed (or expected)
- Monthly minimum debt payments for each debt (you have this information from the balance sheet)

Write down expense categories that do not come every month. Many of these expenses comes each year at about the same time—examples are birthdays gifts, summer camps, or holiday spending. We forget about them when building budgets because we look at the last month to get an idea of what we spent. Each month, you will need to put aside some money for each of these expected future expenses and then spend that money when the time comes. These expenses do not come "out of the blue." They are not emergencies. These are expenses you have to pay—you just don't have to pay them this month. You will save some money toward them each month and will break down the annual amount into the monthly amount needed to save up for the time you need it.

It requires a bit more effort to remember those one-time expenses that seem to come out of the blue, like car repairs, tree trimming, or lawn maintenance. Following is a list of examples of those kinds of expenses.

- Travel expenses
- Summer camps
- Medical expenses
- Birthday parties
- Holiday gifts
- Clothes
- Yard maintenance
- Sports fees
- New car or vehicle purchase
- Others

Fill in these categories with the actual dollar amounts spent each month. This is the beginning of a budget. Start with what you spend now, not what you wish or think you should spend. You need to be aware of your current spending habits before you can focus on new spending habits.

The real work comes in the next step. Decide where you want to and will spend money each month. Make intentional choices about how each dollar goes out of your pocket and into the world. If you don't make these choices, your money will disappear into the wind.

Start with the basics:

- Rent/mortgage
- Home insurance
- Utilities
- Groceries

Then move on to your other categories.

How does it look? Do you have enough money to pay your regular bills, put some toward debts, and still have money left over? Or are you short every month? Do you have more bills to pay and purchases to make without enough money left in the budget? If you are short, the budget is a wake-up call, and it's time to make some changes. We'll talk more about that later.

Ideally, you have money left over. If you do, create a budget category called "savings" and put the extra there on your budget sheet.

Your budget should be zeroed out each month—every dollar will go to a category before you get the money in your hands. That way the spending is simple—you know each month how you will spend your money before it comes into your checking account.

YOU WANT ME TO DO WHAT?

You may have looked at the list above and thought, *How can I possibly figure out how I spent my money last month or over the last six months? I cannot even remember what I paid for a cup of coffee yesterday!*

You need to know how you spend your money. You need to decide how you want to spend your money. And you need to spend your money with intention.

If you cannot figure out where your money goes, then follow this exercise. Take the next two weeks and keep track every penny you spend. Get a notebook. Write down the amount every time you spend any money and what it was for, using your list of budget categories. Do this whether you use cash, a credit card, or a check. Most of us are consistent in our spending, and within a few weeks you will have a good idea of your daily expenses.

Maybe you get coffee and a pastry each morning for breakfast, soup for lunch, and make dinner at home. Your daily eating habits will get picked up within two weeks of shopping and dining out. Your gas or public transportation expenses will be pretty close to average over the next two weeks, and you will be able to change your estimate if something special pops up during that time. The same goes for most of your usual expenses.

During these two weeks, take the time to pull out utility bills, mortgage/rent amounts, phone, TV bills, education bills, and insurance statements.

Now you have most of the information you need to get started on a budget. Nobody gets this right the first time, and you will refine your budget and get better at living with it over the next few months. The key is to start, to take this important step in giving yourself the chance to make a huge difference in your financial life.

BIG INCOME AND NO NEED TO BUDGET?

My speaking and work let me meet with people of different ages, incomes, wealth, and professions. So often, families with larger-than-average incomes do not budget or feel the need to do so. They feel like they have enough money to cover the basics of living and still enjoy the lifestyle they wish—eating out, entertainment, travel, and more.

Do these kinds of people need to budget? Yes, they do!

Over time, I have read so many stories and research articles saying that wealth is no greater for families with high incomes than those with lower incomes. Their balance sheets have bigger numbers of assets but usually come with bigger mortgages and debts. People who earn more spend more, and they often wonder where it all went, just like everyone else. These families often have what looks like a "better" lifestyle with more expensive cars, clothes, and furniture. Unfortunately, they often have balance sheets that show more liabilities than assets, and they feel like they lack time, wealth, and happiness.

Families all along the economic scale need to sit down and make serious decisions about spending—and they need to decide how they want to grab hold of their current income to make sure they can live a comfortable, stress-free life now and in the future.

Families who are a bit more affluent have more wiggle room in working their budgets, but they need to make the same decisions as everyone else—how much of their current income should be saved for emergency funds, future purchases, retirement income, and funding future needs for a family member with special needs?

SOFTWARE TO THE RESCUE

There are amazing tools to use to help you budget and review your spending. Start using one as soon as possible. Quicken and Mint. com are fine examples. Your bank may also provide some kind of budgeting tool. These tools let you download your bank transaction reports and code them by spending category. You can download the last ninety days to see where you have spent your money. Within an hour, you can download the software, set up your bank accounts, and have a clear picture of where you spent money with your debit and credit cards. Cash transactions will show as withdrawals, and checks will need to be reconciled. If you use a debit or credit card for most spending, you will soon have a budget.

Over time and with little work, you'll have created a picture of your spending. You can run a report on your spending over pretty much any time period you choose. These tools can help you track what you spend and help you decide how to adjust or change your spending in the future.

WATCH THESE THREE AREAS

Three costs give families the most trouble if they are not controlled—housing expenses, food, and cars and other vehicles.

Housing Expenses

Financial planners learn a few key ratios over time that help people look at spending. A financial planning rule of thumb says you should not spend more than 35 percent of your take-home pay on your rent or mortgage. Ideally, this number should be at 25 percent or lower. If it is above 25 percent, you will not have money in your budget to live, eat, and pay off debts.

You will have to choose your course of action from here if your house payment is too high. Do you want to move? Do you live in a particular neighborhood for safety and education? Are you underwater on your mortgage, leaving you few choices? Should you look for a second job or some other way to increase your take-home pay? How long can you afford to wait until your income increases?

There are other houses that can provide much of what you like if you cannot afford your house. Consider a move as part of your plan to get your Blueprints in place.

Food

The food budget takes the most work to get under control. We spend more on food as life gets busy and we lack the time to eat at home or prepare our meals. Eating out, getting coffee, picking up drinks on the go, and other such habits all come with a cost much higher than shopping at a grocery store, preparing meals, and planning in advance.

A few years ago I looked at how to cut spending on food in my household without sacrificing quality. A club store opened near me, and I decided to join to see if there was a difference in the amount I spent. I was shocked at my savings on food I was buying anyway. The organic chicken, vegetables, fruit, and bread were all substantially less than the same foods at my grocery store. Packaged items like soap, shampoos, detergent, garbage bags, and more also offered huge savings. I did have to change my behavior a little. Buying a bag of spinach at the wholesale club or a tray of blueberries took commitment so that the food was used and not wasted. It can be easy to buy too much and throw out food; when that happens, the savings go with it. My change in behavior led to big savings.

Many of my clients need to purchase special foods to help maintain and improve the life and health of their family member with special needs. Gluten-free diets cost more than typical diets, for example, and if that's the case for your family, you need to account for this in your grocery and dining budgets.

There is no percentage rule of what a family should spend. You have to remember your commitment. Getting out of debt and beginning to build your assets means making changes in your life. Those changes may involve shopping at a different store, preparing more meals at home, or buying different brands. Small sacrifices today will yield enormous rewards in the future.

Cars and Other Vehicles

The average car payment in the United States is just under $500 per month. The median family income in the United States is about $50,000. This means that on average, more than 10 percent of household income goes to a car. Families with two cars and two car payments could be spending more on their cars than on their mortgage. Last I checked, cars do not usually go up in value.

Are you spending too much on your car and on other vehicles? You need to get out of your car payments and put that money toward other debts and building your savings.

You do not have to have a car payment to own a car. There are cars of every make and model that can be had for any cash budget.

If you have a car payment, sell the car, then pay cash for the cheapest car you can get by with. Save the amount you were making on car payments for even a year and you can quickly upgrade to a better car. Save the amount you were making on payments for one more year, and you can improve your car yet again.

Here's how it works. Let's say you have a $400-per-month car payment. In one year of saving, you will be able to buy a car for $4,800. A $4,800 car is not going to turn heads, but it will do a great job getting you to work, your kids to school, and everyone to the store. Next year, you get to turn in your $4,800 car, add the $4,800 saved in the second year, and get a car worth close to $10,000. You can buy a lot of car for $10,000. Even better, you can wait another year and use that $4,800 to pay off debt.

Boats, motorcycles, RVs, and any other vehicle or toy needs to go if you are in debt. All of these should be bought with cash when you want and can afford them in the future.

SPECIAL-NEEDS EXPENSES

If you have a family member with special needs, you have a whole range of expenses your neighbors and friends do not have. My daughter has music therapy, occupational therapy, and speech therapy each week. She had higher medical expenses throughout her first five years than any of my other children. She requires medication for thyroid issues and an allergy prescription to ward off sinus infections. Your family may have other expenses, like daily medications and supplements not covered by insurance or Medicaid; durable medical equipment like wheelchairs and oxygen; and visits to specialists, therapists, and hospitals.

These expenses can be hard to budget, as they can come out of the blue. You still need to work these into your budget. Review how much you've spent recently and over the past twelve months. Was this a fairly typical year? If so, you will have a monthly budget line that will allow you to save money toward those expenses, since you can assume you will have the same expenses next year. Then there are the atypical, unplanned-for expenses; for example, my daughter had pneumonia while I was writing this book. You will need additional amounts in your emergency fund to cover unplanned expenses—like travel, food, and medical—that may come in the future.

Get these expenses on paper so you can develop a strategy to pay for them as they occur. If you're not prepared, you can get hit with big bills that force you to use credit cards or have unpaid medical costs that keep bill collectors at your door.

Understanding these expenses may help you locate additional sources to pay some of them. As mentioned previously, our local Down syndrome association has a scholarship program that helps defray expenses for families. The State of Colorado has a Medicaid waiver program that picks up costs for families who have workplace health insurance.

 Worksheet: Special-Needs Expenses

SCHEDULE YOUR BUDGET SESSIONS

Each week or month, take time to schedule a budget projection and review. At the beginning, it helps to set a weekly review meeting to see how you've done. You need to practice your budget habit over time to become good at it. It is like a muscle you have not stretched or used for years. It may be painful at first, but you will quickly get the hang of it. You will make mistakes and errors or forget to include expenses when you first start out. Make changes and add these items as you go along.

DO NOT GO IT ALONE

Couples must work together on a budget. You each need to live within the budget and be committed to the goals of getting out of debt, saving for the future, and providing the best life possible for yourself, each other, and each of your family members. You cannot leave a legacy and fund a special-needs trust unless you work together.

"Good luck!" you say.

"No way that'll happen!" you say.

"We never agree with each other about money!"

The couples I work with fall into two categories. One set discusses significant financial issues, something they have done their entire marriage. These people cannot imagine making a financial decision without each other's input. They agree on spending issues and check in with each other on anything bigger than a lunch expense. These couples seem to come from another planet and have worked out their marital roles around finances easily and without friction.

More frequently, couples do not have the ability to sit and make financial decisions together. Life is busy, and financial conversations seem like work. We want to come home to our families and leave the responsibilities of the office behind, play with our kids, be entertained by our spouse, and enjoy our evening. Financial discussions mean making decisions, resolving disagreements, and facing hard choices. It sounds like work.

The following are a few techniques to help you in making financial decisions. Your relationship can become closer if you work together instead of allowing finances to create more conflict.

DEFINE YOUR ROLES AND RESPECT EACH OTHER

Usually, one spouse votes with security and the other with possibility. One is the Record Keeper who needs to know where everything is; the other is the Financial Floater who really just wants to know everything is okay. Each view matters. Blueprints helps you build financial security for your family that will create a life of freedom, independence, and satisfaction for each member of your family.

Security and freedom go hand in hand; they are not in conflict. The budget will include expenses for fun—like vacations, toys for children and adults, entertainment, dining out, and more. But it must first take care of basics, like food, housing, clothing, and utilities. The basics and fun must both be done in order for life to be fulfilling and enjoyable. The budget is not a battle over who gets to do what—it is a map for how you wish to live once you have taken care of the basics and you are out of debt and saving for future needs.

The Record Keeper likes digging into the numbers, creating spreadsheets, and tallying numbers. The Financial Floater has no interest in the calculations and reconciliations—this spouse just wants it to work, know it is working, and have input from time to time.

Decide your roles. Which of you will download information to your budget software, write down the numbers, and track spending? Which spouse will spend more time talking about the future and making sure the family is enjoying life today and focusing on the future? You can both do both, but usually one role fits a particular spouse better.

What works here is that one spouse is charged with handling the family bookkeeping. This spouse writes checks for the mortgage and utilities, balances the checkbook, and opens the bank, retirement, and other investment statements. This spouse likes doing these things most of the time and cannot feel comfortable unless he or she knows that these aspects of life have been done and done right.

The other spouse floats in from time to time and wants to know that finances are in good shape but does not want to get too involved. Taking part in financial decisions creates stress for this person. This spouse needs to be involved in determining the key budget pieces and needs to live with decisions made together.

OWN UP TO YOUR MISTAKES

Living with a budget takes effort. You may have to cook a few more meals or drink coffee at home. You may give up your personal trainer and still need to work out to stay healthy. There will be a thousand temptations as you start down the road of eliminating debt and using your budget. Stores have sales every single day, and you will have to pass on those deals until you decide you have the money to spend on new clothes, shoes, TVs, or toys.

Come to your family budget meeting and review what worked and what did not during the period since you last met. Together, you can work to find solutions. Maybe making coffee in the morning will not work for you every day. It's just one more thing to do as you prepare breakfast, pack lunches, get the kids dressed, and prepare for the day. For you, the drive-through window is an affordable luxury and a necessary way to get the day started. Find something else you can cut if this is the case. Mistakes highlight changes you can make or behaviors you no longer need. Decide which and move on together.

Celebrate Success

Celebrate your budget successes every time you meet. You will always have something positive to discuss in your budget meetings. It may be that you are still sitting down and talking about your budget each month, which you did not do before. It may be you've found a way to save money on gas, groceries, utilities, or insurance—and that money can now be used to reduce debt further or put toward savings.

The celebration does not have to involve money. It can be hugs, a family dance party, an extra glass of wine, or anything else you choose.

Adjust for One-Income Families

Trouble sometimes occurs when one person does not work outside the home and the other brings in the family income. The working spouse may feel a sense of privilege about certain expenses—like lunches out, coffee on the way to work, a certain kind of car—as a way to make it easier to get to work and enjoy the workday. There are going to be work-related expenses that must be covered in the family budget, and these should be agreed to.

In cases where families are working their way out of debt, expenses need to be minimized. The cup of coffee on the way to the office is a four-dollar habit you may need to give up for a few months or years until you are on the path of meeting your family goals. That four-dollar cup of coffee adds up—four-dollars per day over twenty working days is eighty dollars per month, or $960 per year. The average American family earned just more than $50,000 in 2011. Giving up that cup gives the average American family a 2 percent pay raise.

The stay-at-home family member may be spending money on little pleasures to pass the time or for entertainment. This may look like extra nights out with friends, hiring babysitters, trips to the mall or movies, or eating at restaurants that have play places to keep kids entertained.

All of the expenses of the working spouse and stay-at-home spouse are meaningful, useful expenses. The issue for most budgets comes down to which changes you are willing to make today to change your life forever. Can you give up a cup of coffee, a movie, or dining out to set your future on a different path? Do you want these changes to add up to a stable financial future in thirty days, six months, or longer?

You need to decide where your money will go before it comes in, and you need to make changes in your spending habits to reflect those decisions. You need to act in a way that changes your life and the life of your family member with special needs.

FAMILIES OF EVERY INCOME LEVEL MAKE CHOICES

These decisions and behaviors are the same whether you earn $50,000 or $250,000 a year. I have met many people who earn high amounts but have no savings and who are one paycheck away from missing a house payment and financial disaster.

One family I met with had a household income of more than $300,000 but had nothing to show for it when we first met. No money for retirement in a 401k. No emergency fund. Almost no equity in their house. They had the capacity to save but never got around to doing it. Each time the family earned more, they spent more. This family ate out every dinner and every lunch, had the highest monthly cable bill I have ever seen, and pretty much lived as they wished.

They did not feel like they were in a crisis; their only debt was the house, and they could afford their mortgage payments. They did not see or feel the real issues in their financial life. They needed to save 15 percent or more of their income for retirement and put money away for important events and for the needs of their children. They had enough money to live well and did not see the need to be focused about savings. In reality, this family was a few paychecks away from losing everything they had.

They met with me because they were starting to realize they were going to need income and assets for the future if they wanted to retire with the same lifestyle they were enjoying. The first step was to draw up a simple budget and find a few areas they could change. They started putting money into the husband's 401k and began building emergency funds. They started the process of saving and now understand the importance of watching their spending today to live the life they want in the future—a life without financial stress.

BECOME PASSIONATE

Make a choice.

Remain as you are today and continue to live in fear of losing your home, your security, and the ability to enjoy life.

Or make small changes and plod along, taking years to see the benefits of a budget and saving.

Or get excited, get crazy, and make an immediate, impactful difference for you and your family.

Jump in. Go for it. You will amaze yourself by how quickly you can go from feeling like your financial life is out of control to building a life of financial stability and peace. Change the life of your family forever by getting out of debt, saving, and creating assets to care for yourself and your family member with special needs.

PAY OFF DEBTS

Once you establish a monthly budget, you can direct some of your income to pay off debts. A budget gives you an amount each month for debt payments, whether $100, $1,000, or $10,000. The amount you can put toward paying off debt is a mix of how much income you earn and how deeply you want to cut your other expenses. This Building Block should hurt—feeling the pinch today will prevent you from getting into debt in the future.

ORDER YOUR DEBTS

List your debts in order of smallest to largest by amount owed. Do not order them by interest rate—do it by dollar amount. Your interest rate is the least of your concerns right now. Paying off debts and crossing them off your list will help you achieve debt freedom faster than doing it in order of interest rate.

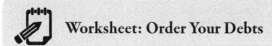

Worksheet: Order Your Debts

Your list should include all the debts you wrote on the liability section of the balance sheet you created earlier. However, the order on the debt-elimination sheet will be different. You need to show the name of each lender, amount owed, interest rate, date started, and minimum payment due each month.

Your budget will show the minimum payment for each debt owed as a line item to be paid each month. In this Building Block, set your budget to pay minimum payments on all outstanding debts.

Review your budget again to see how much extra money you have at the end of each month or pay period, and set it aside for savings.

Yes, savings.

No savings? Take out your pencil and go back to your budget. For now, review expenses you can live without until you pay off your debt. Cable or satellite goes. Dining out costs far more than cooking at home, so it is time to change where you eat. Movies, sporting events, the extra car you keep around and have to insure—all of these are expenses you can cut until you get debt under control. Sell what you don't need, stay home more, and find new ways to entertain yourself.

When you do have extra dollars in your budget, where does that money go? If you still have debt, that money should go to pay off or pay down a debt. If not, put it into a savings account with your primary financial institution. Building Block 6 will help you understand at what point you have enough in your savings account.

Your debt list may look like this:

Owed To	*Balance*	*Rate*	*Min. Pmt*	*Date*	*Pmt Due*
Store charge card	$475	12%	$25	2013	April 15
Credit card	$1,025	17.4%	$75	2011	April 15
Car loan	$6,450	7.5%	$368	2010	April 23
Student loan	$18,543	4.65%	$632	2004	April 4
Mortgage	$236,000	4.25%	$1245	2008	April 9

Use the savings amount from your budget and pay it toward the first debt. For example, say you have savings this month of $250. Pay that to the store charge card of $475. Next month, do the same and you will have paid that debt off. Once your store charge card is paid off, you have an extra $25 on top of the $250, so put that toward the credit card. In a few months, the credit card will be gone, and you will put all those extra payments toward the car loan.

Keep rolling your payments into your debts as you pay each one off. You will build momentum and be on the path to clearing all your debt. Stop the process when all you have left is your mortgage.

The key to paying down debts is to see progress. Your old way of doing it meant ignoring debts, paying the company with the most threatening letters, or sprinkling payments here or there without any thought to how or why. The process above helps you because it is simple to follow, systematic, and gives you the satisfaction of checking off debts paid. You need wins along the way, and paying the small ones first gives you quick wins. You then have more money to put toward the bigger debts, which helps you see progress.

Your next Building Block is to take the amount you paid toward debts and put it into an emergency fund to protect you from a crisis. We'll talk more about that later.

A NOTE FOR PEOPLE STRUGGLING WITH DEBT

Most of the people I work with have debts but have the ability to pay those debts off in a few months or years. They have not focused on the debt but have let it hang around while they spend their money in other ways. They do not see that their debt prevents them from building financial stability.

Others I talk to are truly struggling with debt. They are being harassed by collectors, cannot make progress, and cannot see a path to eliminating debt. They look at bankruptcy as a way out and a way to start over.

If you feel this level of distress, change the way you think about your financial life. Plan to budget and follow the Building Blocks; your budget should start with payments to keep a roof over your head, food on the table, and the lights and heat working. Pay these first every month. Do not pay student loans, credit cards, and other debt payments until you first take care of these basic needs.

Keep it simple. Pay the following first and in this order:

- Food
- Utilities
- Mortgage or rent

It is hard to think straight when you are worried about these three things. Take care of these, and you will begin to be able to address the next issues.

Next, look at your car. Most of us depend on a car to get to work, to shop, and to manage our children's schedules. Make this payment next. You will need to eliminate your car payment by buying a car for cash—a simple car that works well enough to get to work, school, and the store. You may be able to save hundreds each month by trading your current car in for something less expensive.

After the car, take care of other basic family needs, like clothing. Then make minimum payments on everything else. Do not spend money on anything else at this point. Also, do not make payments toward credit cards, student loans, and cars if you cannot feed yourself, keep the lights on, and have a place to live. Your credit score is not as important as taking care of your family today.

MORTGAGE

A mortgage is different from other debts. There is not an immediate need to pay off the mortgage with extra savings once other debts are paid. Before you pay off your mortgage, you should create an emergency fund and put money away for retirement, special-needs expenses, and education. After that, you can decide whether or not you want to pay off your mortgage.

REWARD YOURSELF

Think of a few small rewards to celebrate each accomplishment. Small rewards make a big difference in enjoying the process of budgeting and getting out of debt. You may have the goal of paying off your student loans in three years. Cut your goal into sections and find a reasonable reward for each portion of the goal you reach. It may be eating lunch out, downloading a few songs on iTunes, or getting a massage. Celebrate each milestone with something small that lets you feel the positive impact your change in attitude and behavior is having on you.

Find a way to celebrate—you have put yourself in position to change your life and ensure a high quality of life for your entire family. Even though you have not completely gotten there yet, this is a huge step for you and your family, and you need to enjoy it.

Give Yourself an "Attaboy/girl"

Building Block 5 is designed to add the next level of stability to your financial life.

At this point you can start to envision a time when you can save and invest for the future. You know how much you can pay toward debt each month and calculate the amount of time it will take until you are free—three months, a year, three years. This is exciting. Appreciate the big steps you have taken and feel how much control you have. This feeling will increase every time you make payments and every time you knock out one credit card or student loan.

At this point, you are just beginning to see the results of your planning and dreaming. The foundation is poured and the frame has started going up.

The Blueprints are turning your dreams into reality, but the process takes time. Still, you have taken a big step and need to take a moment to appreciate the work. Progress started when you put together a budget that focused on eliminating debt. And your excitement will increase as you see the debts on your balance sheet disappear and your assets grow.

BUILDING BLOCK 6

Financial Stability

Life feels different when you have no debt. It feels good. It feels like it belongs to you. It feels like you can fearlessly step out in any direction.

Gather up all that energy and thinking you put toward stress and worry. Take a huge breath, and let it out slowly. Congratulate yourself on getting out of debt. Enjoy the moment. Get ready to start living the life you've dreamed.

Take out your DreamList. Now you get to build the financial future that will help you live those dreams. Review the most important goals and take a moment to feel what it will be like for you when are doing what you want to do. Does your DreamList include getting a new car, moving to a new home, investing in yourself in a new career, or having funds to pay for trips and therapies for your family member with special needs? Put yourself in the mindset of knowing you're going to make those dreams happen.

This is the moment you get to work on the DreamList. The DreamList helped you stay motivated to get this far—to put your estate plan in place and pay off your debts. Now the DreamList becomes your motivation to save and invest so you can enjoy life.

Building Block 6 shows a few simple financial techniques that can keep you from getting back into debt. Financial stability comes when you build your savings. You have taken the time to attack and eliminate your debt. You will now have hundreds or thousands of extra dollars each month that used to go for debt payments.

REMEMBER HOW YOU GOT HERE

First, take a moment to look back at how you got into debt so you can learn not to get back there again.

Credit cards. Credit-card debt represents a choice—a choice to finance life instead of paying for it up front. Credit cards helped you buy something you could not afford. There was no money in an account to buy clothes, furniture, entertainment, travel, or whatever else you financed. Those purchases wound up on a card, and the required payments hang around. Those good times cost you 18 percent each year and add stress every time the mail comes.

Medical expenses. You had nothing saved to pay for the medical expenses that arose. A bill came each month for the costs not covered by insurance. Copays. Out-of-network doctors. Unreimbursed costs. Interest costs piled up, and those medical expenses caused continual pain.

Cars. Car loans kept you from saving money. Your cars were sold with affordable payment plans, but the cars themselves were not affordable. People pay too much for cars because payments make them seem affordable. As mentioned, the average car payment for

US citizens is currently just under $500 per month. Families work extra hours just to pay for cars. That's money you should be saving for the future.

Student loans. Student loans seemed like a good idea at the time you took them out. They gave you an education and pathway to a career. Hopefully, your loans gave you a career that earns enough income to pay them off. But you still had the loan even after five, ten, or twenty years. This loan served its purpose at the time but was holding you back.

Upside-down real estate. Everyone said that investing in real estate was a sure thing. The theory was to borrow money against a property with no money down, wait a few years, and sell the property for a killing. That theory stopped working when the real estate market went into a depression. Many people lost their primary homes and rental properties. Borrowing money for rental property is a big risk. Mortgage payments that are too high will crush your spirit.

PREPARE FOR A STABLE FUTURE

The first step in keeping finances strong is to build an emergency fund. You need money sitting in a savings or money market account waiting for the day it's needed. Hopefully, you will never need the money in those accounts.

Second, build an escrow account. This is a second checking or savings account filled with money you put away from each paycheck for expenses that are expected during the next twelve to thirty-six months.

Your goal is to fund these accounts each month and not touch them except when they are needed.

Emergency Funds

Emergency funds are financial insurance. These funds do not grow wealth—they protect your family. These funds will earn little to no interest but are ready to access at a moment's notice.

Build emergency funds after paying off debts other than your house. Basic financial planning suggests that emergency funds hold three to six months of spending needs, not what you would earn during that period. The math is simple: if your family spends $4,000 per month for regular living expenses, then the emergency fund should have between $12,000 and $24,000.

Think what could happen in an emergency, such as losing a job. The earned income goes away when someone is fired or laid off, decides to change careers, or quits. The job loss may be painful, disruptive, a surprise, and difficult to stomach. The emergency fund takes one major stress off you and the family—food, housing, lights, and medical expenses are covered by emergency fund, which lets you weather a tough career moment without turning it into a family crisis.

Medical events create financial emergencies. A friend of mine has a daughter who spent close to a month in the hospital. Medical insurance covered the costs of her care, but it did not cover the expenses the family needed for Mom or Dad to support her in the hospital. This family has two other children, and they needed to hire care providers to feed the other children and get them to school, sports, and other activities. The family also had other costs, including transportation to the hospital and hotel stays near the hospital. These were unexpected family costs that could have created a financial disaster if they'd had to use credit cards or borrow against their home. Instead, their emergency funds allowed them to focus on the health issues and on healing without the additional financial stress.

Building Your Emergency Fund

The emergency fund starts when you take the money you were using to pay your debts and direct it toward savings. Set up a new savings or money market account. Do not mix this money with your checking account. The emergency fund should be more difficult to access than writing a check or using your debit card. You do not want these funds to disappear in a spending frenzy one day at the mall or when you are online. This fund will build quickly as you take the money you used to send to debtors and instead keep it for yourself.

One of my clients pays close to $1,200 per month toward credit-card debt. The debt just sat and never seemed like a problem. She would add to it and make payments, but she never got around to zeroing out the balance. She had the income to pay off the cards but just never focused on it. We recently met and came up with a plan for her to pay off all of her credit cards over the next eighteen months by having her pay $2,000 per month toward the cards. She will use any bonuses or extra income she gets as extra lump-sum payments to the cards. Her next step will be to put that $2,000 per month in her emergency fund, which will cover three months of expenses in next to no time once those credit card payments go into her own savings account.

By far the biggest question people ask has to do with how much they can expect to earn on an emergency account. Remember the purpose of this account—it is insurance against catastrophe. Usually with insurance, you pay something for the benefit. Car, home, health, and life insurance come at a monthly cost. An emergency fund insures you against financial problems, and you do not have to pay a dime for it. Your investments will earn money for you and are covered in the next Building Block.

Keep emergency funds in bank accounts or money-market funds. The goal is simple access, not rate of return.

Using Your Emergency Fund

Emergency funds are not meant to be used for expenses you know are coming. Birthday presents are not emergencies. School clothes are not emergencies. Summer camps and sports fees are not emergencies. These are regular expenses—even if they only show up once a year.

True emergencies are things like car tires blowing out. Leaks in the roof. Unexpected medical emergencies. Travel expenses to care for a family member in crisis. You cannot see these things coming; they do not show up on the calendar each week, month, or year.

Let's look at an example from my own experience. My refrigerator recently broke down, and I had to buy a new one. I had money set aside in an emergency fund and bought a new refrigerator. Was I happy about it? No. The old refrigerator seemed fine. I was not expecting to replace it. I hate shopping. But the emergency fund did what it was supposed to do—it kept me from financing a refrigerator and paying 8 to 12 percent of the cost over the next three years.

The purchase, replacement, and installation of my new refrigerator were all a minor headache, but it did not cause me any financial stress. The money was there, ready to go.

Now my emergency fund has less money in it, but I still need the fund. I still need it to contain at least three to six months of reserves. So what do I have to do? I have to hit the pause button on spending or investing until the emergency fund is once again full. Funding can come from reducing contributions to retirement accounts, eating at home more, going out less, or from some other place in my budget.

How Many Months Works Best?

The minimum amount you need in an emergency fund is what you would spend in a three-month period. Financial planners recommend three to six months of spending money. So how much should you have?

Families with stable incomes can get by with lower amounts in their emergency funds. Teachers, police officers, and members of the military have high degrees of job security and predictable incomes.

They are not likely to get fired, have jobs disappear overseas, or see big cuts in pay. Do you fit this mold? Do you think you can predict that your job will be similar or better over the next few years? If so, a smaller emergency fund can work for now.

Many of my clients have unpredictable incomes. They work in sales jobs, own businesses, are professionals (such as lawyers and doctors), or are independent contractors. They do not know if next month's income will be the same as this month's. They do not know from year to year how much income they will earn. Those with unpredictable incomes or changing careers will need to have larger amounts saved in their emergency funds to smooth over any unexpected issues.

Building Your Escrow Accounts

In addition to emergency funds, families need to have escrow accounts.

Your main bills get paid as they come—you send a check to your mortgage company, landlord, utility company, and phone company each month. These expenses show up on the budget each and every month.

What do you do about bills that get paid "every so often"? Families do not have to go to the doctor each month. They also don't buy presents for holidays and birthdays every month. There needs to be money set aside to meet these expenses. There should also be an account holding money to pay for vacations, summer camps, and sports fees. Bigger ticket items or seasonal activities need to be funded today even though they will not be paid for months or years.

The best way to handle these infrequent expenses is to put aside money in an escrow account and then keep track of how you plan to spend that money. Set up a new account for the escrow reserves; you may use a new checking or savings account. Take money dedicated to the expenses that do not show up each month and move it from your regular checking account to your escrow account.

For instance, maybe you pay a garbage company once every three months. This bill will not be a surprise; it is not an unexpected emergency. You need to pay this bill if you want your garbage taken away. If do not pay it, there will soon be a huge pile of garbage behind your house. That's a pretty simple concept: save some money to pay the bill, or have a big pile of garbage. Break this payment into a monthly expense and put that monthly expense on your budget worksheet. Take the money and move it into the escrow account, where it will sit until you need it for your garbage bill. Move the money from the escrow account to your checking account when the bill needs to be paid. Then start saving again for this bill, which will come due again in three months.

This example is a small way of showing how an escrow account works. We have lots of future expenses to save for—new cars, house down payments, medical costs, family gifts, summer camps, and travel. We may know how much a future need will be, such as the fee for next year's summer camp. Or we can estimate for things like medical expenses and clothing—expenses we know we will have but don't know the amount or timing for.

If you have been using a program to track your spending, you should be able to run a report that shows what you spent last year on certain items. Run a report of what you paid for medical to get an idea of your prior year's spending. Escrow one-twelfth of that each month to build a medical fund to pay for those expenses as they come.

Building escrow funds can take time. You may have decided to set aside $100 per month for medical expenses after reviewing your last year. Last year may have looked something like this:

5 copays for physician visits ($30 each equals $150)
1 emergency room visit ($250 out of pocket)
6 dental visits ($100 each equals $600)
Glasses and eye appointments ($200)

In this example, $1,200 was spent over the past twelve months for medical expenses. The escrow account starts with $100 put aside each month to cover these expenses. You may have to use this money or more next month if you have an emergency-room visit, or you may have a few months to build the fund and spend as needed. Either way, start the discipline of putting some money away each month. This step will put you in the driver's seat in protecting your assets, stop you from using credit cards to cover shortfalls, and help start the process of building your wealth.

Use this same process for any expenses you know will come in the future. Do you plan to buy a car in two years? Break up the cost into twenty-four payments and save that in your escrow account each month. Will you need new hearing aids? Find out the expected cost, and save each month to have the cash ready to buy them when the time comes. This works for any expense that will not come out of your income in the current month.

STABILITY

Emergency funds and escrow accounts provide financial stability. This Building Block keeps you moving in the right direction. You do not take a giant step backward into debt if you have the money when you need it.

BUILDING BLOCK 7

Protect Your Family

Think about the last house you saw being built. The work on a house moves quickly from foundation to frame once the plans are in place, the permits are pulled, and the contractor is hired. You saw the land cleared, a foundation put together, and the framing go up. At some point, you began to see what the house would look like. And yet the construction process couldn't continue safely since there was the threat of damage from rain, hail, snow, and wind. There was no roof and nothing to protect the structure. Like this house, your Blueprints plan cannot go forward without several key, protective elements in place.

The next Building Block in the Blueprints process acts like a roof for your family. You will need to have the right types of insurance in the right amounts to protect your family from the potential damage

131

caused by unforeseen events. Insurance coverage will adapt over time as your needs change.

The insurances protecting your family must be put in place as soon as you begin getting out of debt. At first, some of your insurance coverage will seem like the big blue makeshift tarp covering the framing of a roof—it will look a little ragged. And it will be temporary. Over time, you will replace or add to your coverage as needed.

Building Block 7 shows you the type of life insurance you need for special-needs planning. It also shows you how to protect your family from the effects of unemployment, disability, and the costs of long-term care.

The income coming into your household is the single biggest tool you have to create wealth, retire comfortably, and pay for the future needs of your loved one with special needs. This income stream stops if you cannot work for some reason—including your own disability. The income stops if you die during your working years as a result of an accident, heart attack, or some other cause. The income stops if you get laid off, your employer closes the business, or you leave your job.

Make sure you have protection for three areas at this point: death, loss of a job, and disability. Long-term care insurance is an important part of the protection plan for families following the Blueprints steps. Even though we discuss it here as an important protection piece, you should wait to buy this insurance until you are finished with the other Building Blocks.

LIFE INSURANCE

Families just starting the Blueprints process need life insurance.

Do not leave your family unprotected. A death is tragedy enough for a family; have some financial protection in place to smooth the time of grief and loss. There is only one type of insurance to buy at this stage: term life insurance.

Life insurance pays your estate (your family, a trust, or anyone you choose) when you die. It pays without any income taxes taken out. Buy this insurance to protect your family against the loss of the income you bring home and to pay off debts (if you have not yet finished Building Block 5).

You owe it to your family to have insurance in place. This provides incredible peace of mind against the worst possible scenario—the untimely death of someone in your family.

Do not leave your family in extreme financial risk. Buy the simplest, least expensive type of policy available, which is term life insurance. At this point, there are very few times where any other type of life insurance makes sense. Do not buy anything called "whole life," "indexed life," "universal life," or any other type of "permanent insurance" at this point. You are building and accumulating wealth. Term life insurance covers your family through the time it takes to do this.

The death benefit of a life-insurance policy cannot replace the love, activity, spirit, and role of a family member who dies. Dad or Mom cannot be replaced. Grieving is a process that takes time, and those initial days, weeks, and months are difficult. The family must first process the loss and feel the pain associated with it. Families do not need additional stress during this time, especially stress that can be avoided. Money from a life-insurance policy provides financial security and alleviates worry about the ability to make mortgage payments, pay for school, buy clothes, and provide food.

Each adult family member needs to have life insurance. Some families have two working spouses, and each has income that needs to be replaced. Others have a stay-at-home family member, and the financial value of that family member must be replaced. Day care, home-health assistance, transportation, and other various aspects of daily life will need to be taken over by a nanny, driver, nurse, or therapist.

Life insurance comes in two basic categories—term insurance and everything else. There are a few basic decisions to make when buying a term insurance policy, and it will help for you to think through the decision before meeting with a financial adviser or insurance broker. The two biggest decisions are how long should the coverage should last and how much benefit is needed.

TERM INSURANCE

Term insurance covers you for a specified period of time—a term. This insurance can be bought for terms of ten, fifteen, twenty, or thirty years. You decide how much insurance you want when you apply for a policy. You can get $100,000, $250,000, $1,000,000, or more—or any amount in between.

Today's policies are usually bought as level term policies. You pay the same amount each year during the time you hold the policy through the end of the term. For example, your premium may be $60 per month, $250 per year, or $1,000 every three months. The policy remains in place as long as the premium gets paid up to the amount of time purchased.

The premium can be paid monthly, quarterly, or annually, and you choose this when you apply for the policy. This schedule can be changed later. Usually there is a small discount when premiums are paid annually.

The amount of death benefit does not change with a term policy. You start with an initial death benefit or face amount—for example, $500,000. This death benefit amount is the same whether an insured person dies a year after the policy is enacted or eighteen years later, as long as the premium is paid.

The premium charge is based on a combination of factors: the amount of coverage, the length of the term, whether a person smokes, and overall health. You apply for coverage based on the amount of death benefit and time period needed. The insurance company determines health status based on underwriting questions and a review of medical history. They price the policy based on those factors. A healthy thirty-five-year-old getting a $500,000 twenty-year term policy will pay less for the same coverage than a thirty-five-year-old smoker with health problems.

How Long a Term?

Twenty years is the most common length of term insurance for people starting on the Blueprints process. The idea is that you have twenty years to reduce debt, pay off the mortgage, build emergency funds, and make significant progress toward saving for future goals like retirement and special-needs trusts. Twenty years from now, you will not have debt (except maybe a small balance on your mortgage), and there will be funds in investments. Young families may need to have insurance in place for thirty years as they seek to build assets and if they expect to increase their family size.

Many of our clients end up with several term insurance policies. We "ladder" term policies as needs progress: the first twenty-year policy is kept, and a new one added as income increases.

How Much Insurance Should You Get?

Life insurance provides a defined amount of death benefit. You choose how much coverage you want when you apply for a policy. You can get just about any dollar amount you want and can afford (up to a maximum level based on a multiple of your income and other factors).

There are two ways to determine the amount of coverage you need.

1. *The rule of thumb.* An industry rule of thumb says you need somewhere between seven and ten times your income. If your income is $70,000, then you need $490,000 to $700,000 of coverage. Buy what you can afford based on your budget, and get the higher amount if possible. This rule of thumb works well most of the time and gives you a starting point in pricing insurance and getting adequate coverage.

2. *Financial analysis.* The better method involves a detailed financial analysis that includes reviewing the goals you have for the term insurance. You will need to answer the following questions:

- Do you want the insurance to fully pay off debts, including a mortgage?
- Will insurance proceeds fund all or a portion of education expenses?
- How much of the policy will be used to add money to a trust?
- Will the surviving spouse or partner return to work if not working now?
- What living changes will occur if one person passes away?
- What rate of return can you expect on the lump-sum benefit provided by the insurance benefit?

This method means looking at your current financial situation (which you have detailed already) and making choices about which expenses or future costs to fund with insurance in case of an unexpected death. It won't take long for your financial adviser to put these numbers together once you have thought through the purpose of insurance.

Keep the insurance in place even if the premium feels like wasted money. No one likes paying insurance premiums. We hope to pay premiums and never collect on the death benefit—because that means we are healthy, safe, and alive.

One client of mine complains about paying her premium each year. From time to time, she needs a little reminder of why she has the insurance in place. The policy is designed to protect her family if she passes away early. It is there to provide tax benefits and to help her family keep the family business. The premium is the cost of protecting her family and is inexpensive compared to the costs her family would incur if she died without the insurance. We have this conversation every so often, and it helps make the decision to write the premium check easier for her each year as she remembers its purpose.

Don't Buy Too Little

Unfortunately, families often buy less insurance than they need. Ten times the family income looks like a lot when you write that number down, and many people cannot imagine ever needing all that money. Unfortunately, ten times your salary does not look like enough when someone passes away and that income is lost.

There are immediate expenses when someone passes away. Funeral costs. Extra home care. Job training. Family travel. These expenses use a portion of the funds. In addition, the money from a death benefit must replace the income of the person who was working to pay basic living expenses for many years. People underestimate the lifetime value they create by working or taking care of family members.

Many families look to insurance to pay off debt and nothing else. They think of the insurance as a way to clean up past mistakes. These families forget that debt is only one reason to have life insurance. Income replacement is the more important reason. A family cannot live without the income contributions of a working spouse and must create assets that generate income replacement.

OTHER TYPES OF LIFE INSURANCE

There are other types of life insurance. Do not use any of these types of insurance at this stage in the Blueprints process. Most families following the Building Blocks will never need or use the other types of life insurance, usually called "permanent insurance." These types have names like "whole life," "universal life," "variable life," "variable universal life," or "indexed universal life." They all seek to combine some form of an investment account with life insurance and are lousy investment vehicles almost every time.

There are plenty of salespeople who target families who have members with special needs to buy these types of insurance policies. I have yet to see a policy sold to a special-needs family that works for the family. The higher premiums mean that families do not buy enough death benefit, and these policies never seem to create the cash values or investment returns families need over the long term.

These types of policies are sold to families who have members with special needs with the intention of funding a special-needs trust. They do not take into account debt, retirement, and the other needs of the family. The last Building Block of the Blueprints process shows you how to fund a trust and which assets to use. Do not use potential cash value life insurance to fund a special-needs trust until you have every other Building Block in place and have had these in place for many years.

INSURANCE GONE BAD

A woman came into my office for a review of her insurance and to discuss special-needs planning. She had been sold a "permanent" insurance policy to fund a trust for her daughter about ten years before. The insurance salesperson did not have a financial planning background and sold expensive "permanent" insurance policies.

His tool kit had one tool. There were no Building Blocks in place; there was no process to help her. There was only sales pressure.

The woman had a problem when she came to me: she could not afford the premiums. Her income had changed due to a divorce.

Her goal was to leave all her assets to a special-needs trust to benefit her daughter. The woman owned a house, had a significant investment portfolio, and had this insurance policy with more than $300,000 in cash value. On paper, it looked like she was in a good position to live her life comfortably and leave an inheritance to support her daughter.

In reality, she did not have the cash flow to pay the premiums of $30,000 per year for the rest of her life.

She had to make a choice. She had to drastically change the way she lived or change something about her life insurance policy.

We looked closely at the policy to see what had happened. For one, the woman had earned next to nothing inside the policy. She did not get the 10-percent rate of return the stock market had earned over that period of time. She did not get the 6-percent rate of return of the bond market. She did not even get the 2.5-percent rate of return she would have earned in a bank account over that period of time. Her earnings were basically zero. She had the money she put in but little else. She had purchased the policy with the expectation of returns that never materialized. In fact, her money would have made more sitting in a bank account over the same period of time. These types of policies have the potential for tax-free build-up of earnings, yet this tax feature did not add any value. This policy did nothing for her and her family.

The death benefit in this policy was about $1 million, and the intention was to use the death benefit to fund the special-needs trust. The premium each year was about $30,000. In ten years, the policy cash value was close to $300,000. The client was not too old and could be expected to live more than twenty more years when we met. In thirty years, she would have paid close to $900,000 in premiums for a policy that would pay the trust $1,000,000.

Let's put it simply: all this policy did was provide a place for her to keep her cash. If she'd put 90 percent of that money in a bank CD and 10 percent into other investments, she could have had far more money to fund the special-needs trust.

Now let's take a realistic look at her policy: she had next to no access to the cash, she earned less than what her money would have earned in the bank, and she could no longer afford the premiums. The solution? We found a different policy that could still fund the trust and that would not require an additional premium. We were able to salvage her bad situation—but she would have been far better off saving the money outside insurance and investing at least a portion of it to create more value over time.

I still cannot figure out who would consider this a good deal and why there are agents all over the country selling the same types of policies every day to families with special needs.

Stick with term life insurance if you want to protect your family during you're your working years. Then grow your wealth by saving and investing your money outside your insurance policies.

PROTECTING AGAINST UNEMPLOYMENT

Companies close, industries change, and people need to move. These and other reasons may cause you to be unemployed. Unfortunately, too many people treat government-sponsored unemployment coverage like a type of insurance—but it is not dependable. The emergency funds you have in your savings account provide more certain "insurance." The emergency fund supports your family and replaces lost income during times of unemployment. It takes care of your family during times when you are temporarily out of work and covers family living expenses for three to six months. This fund is the best coverage you can have for taking care of your family. You control the emergency fund and do not have to depend on the government when you most need the money.

No one who has an emergency fund wants to use it. It takes time to save up. It requires sacrifice—not dining out, going to movies, taking vacations, or buying more clothes. The key is that the money is there, ready to use should you need it.

Losing a job counts as one of the situations in which you may need to use your emergency fund. Without the fund, you would be forced to live on expensive credit cards and to look for the quickest job you can get to pay the bills. With the fund, you buy yourself time to think and to plan. Your life, career, and family are too important to take a lousy job just to pay the bills. An emergency fund gives you time to plan and a chance to make choices.

Do not depend on government-funded unemployment insurance. Yes, this type of coverage does provide a safety net and may be an additional help at some point. Any extra income makes life easier as you go through the process of changing jobs or careers and take the time to focus on a résumé, network, and apply for a new job. But remember, you might not receive any unemployment benefit from the government. Every state is different in how benefits are earned and delivered, and it is harder in some than others to collect unemployment. States like mine favor employers, and unemployment claims are less likely to be approved than in states like California or New York.

Choices fly out the window if you do not have an emergency fund. At some point, you may decide you can no longer work with your current employer or that you need to move to be close to family so you can take care of parents or get help with your children. Families with emergency funds can plan their next steps, take a few extra weeks or months to make arrangements, and then jump into the next position. Families without emergency funds find themselves forced to take whatever job is open just to pay the bills.

DISABILITY INSURANCE

Insurance industry statistics indicate that a person is more likely to become disabled than die during a working life. This holds true regardless of age. Few people really think of themselves in terms of becoming disabled—we tend to see ourselves as healthy enough to work and healthy enough to work for a long time. We may be worn out from the work we do, fed up with our career path, and exhausted at the end of the day from balancing work life, children, and other obligations, but we usually see ourselves as getting up and being able to do it again tomorrow.

Families with a member with special needs understand how difficult it is to find a job or career path for a person with a physical or intellectual/developmental disability. But that's not the only kind of "disability." Disability has many causes: Complications from giving birth or from pregnancy. Stress-related illness as a result of certain kinds of work. Accidents from activities not related to work, such as skiing, driving, playing soccer, doing yard work, moving heavy boxes, and more. Sadly, the work world does not have many on-ramps for people with disabilities.

You can buy insurance to protect yourself against the loss of income in the event of a disability. This insurance can be bought through your employer if they offer it as a benefit or on an individual basis if not.

The Blueprints process shows you how to build an emergency fund and how important these funds are in creating stability in your financial life. As mentioned, you need to have at least three months of living expenses sitting in an account (at a bank, brokerage firm, or credit union); six months of living expenses is ideal.

The Blueprints process provides your family with protection if you have a short-term disability as the emergency fund provides cash for a few weeks or more. Short-term disability insurance can provide additional protection. But while short-term disability insurance is nice to have, it's not necessary as you accomplish Building Block 6 and have an emergency fund in place. Once your emergency fund is in place, however, you should get long-term disability insurance.

Disability insurance comes in two different types—long- and short-term.

Many disabilities are short-term. For example, you may wind up in the hospital with a broken leg or heart attack and not be able to work for several months. You plan to go back to work as soon as your injury heals and you recover.

Short-term disability policies pay benefits for thirty to ninety days. Such a policy is used to pay part of your income if you become temporarily disabled; such coverage is not meant to last for the rest of your life.

Long-term disability pays when you have a more serious or permanent disability, such as a brain injury, perhaps from a car accident, or loss of eyesight, perhaps from a workplace injury. This insurance usually requires a waiting period ("elimination period") before it will start paying out. Waiting periods usually are thirty, sixty, or ninety days (the most common), but can be as long as a year. The policy pays to replace lost income.

You need to have long-term disability insurance in place for your family. Your emergency fund covers you for the three months you miss work while you wait for the benefits of a long-term policy to start.

Insurance companies offer lower prices the longer the elimination period. This gives the insured person time to heal and recover from any incident before payments begin. A broken leg that takes two months to heal does not trigger disability insurance payments. In such a case, the ninety-day elimination period protected the insurance company. Because the insurance company is less likely to have to pay on a ninety-day elimination period than a thirty-day period, they are willing to pass that savings along.

For those with emergency funds, the waiting period is a time full of uncertainty—medical issues may not resolve quickly, and there is fear of not being able to resume life (job, hobbies, and time with family). The emergency fund buys time, patience, and sanity as you work through difficult issues. The right long-term disability insurance also buys peace of mind, as you know your family will not be forced to move, run up credit cards, or become destitute if the disability remains.

The first place to look for disability insurance is with employers. Group disability insurance plans are usually less expensive for the same coverage than are individual policies. Like health insurance, insurance companies look at the whole group of people in a company and decide how to charge. They reduce their risk by the large number of people in the company.

Usually, companies that offer group policies do not require applicants to go through any special underwriting process. Employees sign up for coverage with the rest of their benefits. The company will deduct some amount from each paycheck for the coverage.

The benefit paid to you will change depending on who pays the premium. If the employer pays, then disability insurance payments to you will be taxable. Ideally, you pay for this coverage with a payroll deduction. If you pay the premium, the payments are tax free. Most people never stop to complain when an employer or anyone else picks up the check. And if your employer will pay for your insurance, don't stop them from doing it. Chances are you do not have a choice with employer-sponsored coverage—they give you the benefit and pay the premium, or they give you the option to buy and you pay the premium. Take it either way.

If your company does not make coverage available, look for an individual policy to replace a portion of your income.

IMPORTANT COVERAGE AS YOU AGE

Families who have members with special needs should have one more type of insurance: long-term care insurance.

We live in an era where more and more, aging parents are caring for adult children with developmental disabilities. Parents who are now in their seventies and eighties never expected to have their adult child with disabilities living at home. They did not expect their sons and daughters to be alive and doing well. Now these parents are not only facing for caring for a child with special needs but are looking at their own need for supported care. They are looking at having services delivered at home or moving to assisted living and other care facilities.

The costs are not small. The average semiprivate room in a decent location in Colorado costs about $7,500 per month. And the costs keep going up each year.

Costs associated with long-term care can be paid from investment and retirement assets, or they can be funded by the use of insurance. Long-term care insurance offers seniors a way to make sure there is some funding in place for their own continued quality of life and health needs.

Families with a member with special needs should buy long-term care insurance. This insurance protects any assets dedicated to funding a trust.

The types of long-term care insurance change every few years, and you will want to discuss this with your financial planner to make sure you get the type of policy best suited for your family. Consider buying long-term care insurance between the ages of fifty and sixty. You cannot get insurance if you have certain medical conditions, so you will want to start looking at the younger end of the spectrum if you have a family history that could stop you from getting coverage.

LOVE OF YOUR FAMILY

Protect your family against the unexpected events of life. The Beatles sang "Can't Buy Me Love," but you can show love to your family by protecting them in some way from the unexpected. Insurance—life, long-term care, and disability—protects your family from the loss of income and you against having to drain your assets.

Money is needed when you die during your working years and before you have built your assets. Income is needed from the assets of a life-insurance policy or from the payment of a disability policy when you cannot work. Your family will not suffer additional stress and worry about losing a house, losing a car, and being unable to put food on the table when you have the right types of insurance in place.

BUILDING BLOCK 8

Invest for Your Future

Can a teacher become a millionaire?

That question was answered in 2005 when a Canadian elementary school teacher named Roberta Langtry died and left almost $4 million to the Nature Conservancy of Canada.

She never earned a huge salary. She did not own a big business. She did not get stocks options in a tech company. So how did she do it?

Simple: Roberta Langtry spent less than she earned and invested her money in a mix of stocks and bonds. Articles written about Roberta Langtry reveal that she bought government bonds and a mix of high-quality stocks she held on to for a long time.

The Blueprints process shows you how to decide what is important in your life, how to get out of debt, and how to start saving for the future. Once you have finished the first seven Building Blocks, you are in the driver's seat, with the power to accumulate wealth. Your savings will be invested to create wealth for you and your family. You are out of debt, you have an emergency fund, and you are building your future.

With the types of investments you'll start in Building Block 8, you'll start building for your future. That money can be used in a number of ways. Roberta Langtry left her money to a nonprofit organization. Families with special needs look to fund trusts to care for their sons or daughters. Imagine being able to leave almost $4 million in a trust. This should give you peace of mind as you create the quality of life you want for your family.

Bill Gates. Warren Buffett. John D. Rockefeller. The millionaire next door. These people share a common trait—they have created wealth and maintained their wealth over time by investing their savings to grow their asset base.

Building Block 8 shows you how to invest part of your savings to fund future needs, such as retirement income, future special-needs expenses, education accounts, a legacy for your family, and charitable giving.

A WORD ABOUT INVESTING

Do you see yourself as an investor? Are your family messages ones about the dangers of investing or about the value of investing? Before committing money to investments like stocks or bonds, mutual funds, or index funds, take a moment to look inside and understand how you think about investing.

Does it make you nervous?

Do you think there are better things to do with money than put some away for the future?

Do you expect your money to make even more money?

Have you invested and seen growth in your accounts?

We are not born investors. It takes time to become an investor and to understand how investments work.

For so many, the first act of saving is a hard one. They have been programmed by advertising to spend. They model their families' financial turmoil. They hear from their peers that the world is coming to an end. They can't see the need for putting money into investments they may never see or use.

Investing success requires patience, diligence, and time. There is a leap of faith when putting money into an account and expecting there to be more money there in the future. It goes against what too many people have been trained to do—spend, spend, spend. And then spend some more.

The world seems stacked against people who are trying to learn to invest. Turn on the TV. Open a newspaper. Listen to the radio. Check out the home page of Yahoo, MSN, or any other media site. Within a few moments, reports about the economy, stock market, interest rates, housing prices, and related information jump out. Financial news is everywhere. Unfortunately, so much of that financial news shouts out the worst of the stories.

The media bias tends to emphasize the negative. Headlines scream "Markets Fall!" when the stock market is down. When the market recovers the next day, the story is tucked away somewhere on page 10. Economic news, even in a booming economy, talks about unemployment (rather than employment), risk (rather than potential), and regulation (rather than innovation and expansion). Do not get caught up in the negative stuff—and don't let it stop you from investing for the long term.

Also, families are too often a poor source of knowledge about investing. Many families do not talk about money at all. Others talk only about the problems, like how Aunt Mary lost it all during the

Great Depression instead of how Uncle Joe retired comfortably by investing throughout his career.

How have the family stories you grew up with influenced your thoughts about investing? If they are negative, you need to focus on changing your mindset to learn how investing can help you. Even today, years after the financial crisis of 2008/2009, I hear from people how they lost money in the markets and never got it back. The real story is different. Investors who had money in stocks and bonds and who kept it there made money in their portfolios.

This Building Block will guide you through the decisions about which types of accounts to use, the types of investments you need in your portfolio, how to hire the right kind of financial adviser, and how to target a savings amount to use for retirement and funding a trust.

There are many decisions to make as you start investing your money to create wealth. What kind of return and income should you expect from your money? How do you go about investing it in the right types of accounts and in the right types of investments to build the assets you need? How long should this take?

This Building Block has four distinct sections: reasons to invest, the types of toolboxes you need to hold your investments, the tools—types of investments—to use, and some basic investing concepts.

WHY INVEST?

It is easy to understand why people become confused about investing. There are close to 3,200 stocks listed on the New York Stock Exchange. There are thousands of mutual funds owning everything from stocks to bonds to gold to real estate to natural gas. There are CDs, money-market funds, fixed annuities and insured accounts, and more, all designed to hold your cash savings. You can put money in bank accounts, brokerage accounts, a bunch of different types of trusts, and various kinds of retirement accounts—IRA, SEP IRA, Roth IRA, 401(k), 493(b), SARSEP, Simple IRA, 457 plan, and more. The combination of account types, investment types, and strategies out there is enough to make a person dizzy.

So why invest? We invest for one simple reason: to have the money we save earn money.

Investing is a beautiful, magical machine designed to increase your assets. You do not have to go to your office, sign in at work, rake leaves, dig a ditch, write a report, sit in meetings, or take anyone's temperature. You simply let your money do the work, and it provides income and assets in the future.

Imagine an account where you have $100,000 ready when you need it. That sounds like a lot of money; in fact, it's more than the average family has saved for retirement. There are two paths to creating an account with money in it. One is to save it in a bank; that's the slow way. The other way is to save, then invest for growth. This can speed up the amount you have later.

It will take twenty years to save $100,000 in a bank account if you put $5,000 a year away. If you invest the same amount in a moderate-growth portfolio, you will have $100,000 in half that time. Investing helps you accumulate money faster.

Each month, you have two choices with your savings: spend it or save it. Spending feels good—you get new shoes, a new toy, or some other fun thing you want, and you get it now. But saving and investing your money gives you a future—a future filled with the shoes, cars, toys, vacations, medical expenses, and everything else you will need and want without having to keep working every single day for the rest of your life. It will also help pay for the future expenses of your family member with special needs.

This chapter will provide a simple, effective breakdown of how you can take steps to choose which type of account to use and how to invest over time. They are basics that work for most people most of the time.

Find a good financial planner to work with on your investments. A good financial planner will help keep you on track, educate you about the markets, and partner with you in improving your investment strategies and emotional responses to the markets.

WHY WE INVEST: A REAL EXAMPLE

Jane and John (not their real names) came into my office for financial planning help. Jane's mother had passed away, and they were trying to figure out how to handle their inheritance. They were nervous about making a mistake—nervous about handling a legacy gift they never expected to receive.

Jane and John had worked hard their whole lives, owed nothing on their cars, owed little on their house, and had some money saved in retirement accounts. They wondered if they would be able to retire comfortably and were concerned about how to handle the inheritance.

Jane and John had no context for the inherited money. It was about twice the amount they had saved on their own, and they got the entire sum all at once. It created as much stress as it did any sense of relief, as they were now responsible for a lump sum of cash in a brand-new way.

So where should they start? Put the money into a mutual fund? Keep it in cash in a bank account? Pay off their remaining mortgage? Or spend it on a whirlwind trip around the world?

First they needed a financial plan, a way to understand their financial priorities. They needed a DreamList. This DreamList needed to include how much they'd need to live on comfortably for the rest of their lives. They needed to put together their balance sheet and income statement.

For Jane and John, the inheritance was enough to change their future. They had not saved enough for retirement. The inheritance was enough to fill this gap in their planning, but only if they invested some of the money for growth.

Leaving the money in a bank would not provide enough to keep pace with inflation and provide the income they needed. The money would have to grow to help them achieve their goals. They needed to invest in a moderate-growth portfolio to provide them with financial security.

From my perspective as a financial planner, the process of investing for this couple looked easy. A balanced portfolio invested in a mix of US and international stocks and bonds should provide income and growth over time. They did not need to shoot for the stars.

From their perspective, the world seemed like a mess. Politicians in Washington were creating trouble, the Chinese economy was not doing well, interest rates were rising, and the headlines were all doom and gloom. They could not see how their money could earn anything. They were afraid of losing the inheritance the moment they invested it.

Investing requires that people manage their emotions so they will do the right thing to accomplish goals. Jane and John needed to take steps to reduce the emotion involved in investing. For them, this meant keeping a larger-than-usual emergency fund. It meant paying off the mortgage. It meant taking time to invest the money so they could build their wealth slowly. It meant going to investing education classes to learn more.

This couple needed to invest to maintain their standard of living. Investing would provide them with the asset growth and income they needed to live comfortably. If they didn't invest, they would have to sacrifice—move into a smaller house, take fewer vacations, drive older cars, stay home more often for dining and entertainment, and have other decreases in their quality of life.

HOW MUCH TO SAVE AND INVEST

Your budget tells you how much you earn, how much you spend on living expenses, how much to put toward debt, how much to escrow for future expenses, and how much is left over to save and invest.

Once the debts other than the mortgage are paid off, it is time to focus on saving for the future. It's time to add new budget items. One line item will be for retirement savings. Another will be an amount to fund a special-needs trust. There may be more. Savings for college or other educational expenses for children or grandchildren is one. Look back at your DreamList. What other goals will require money? If you have a goal to start a business, buy a vacation home, own rental real estate, travel around the world, or donate to charity, create a savings line for each goal in the budget.

Saving for future goals can be as easy as opening an investment account with your financial adviser. In some cases, like retirement funding, the government has special account options to help improve your ability to save enough for retirement. The special options, or account types, are the tool kits for saving. The investments are the tools you use.

This Building Block does not cover every goal on your list. We will discuss three because they have special reasons and account types: retirement, special-needs trust funding, and education.

WHY WE INVEST: RETIREMENT INCOME

Building Block 8 starts with retirement because each and every one of us must have money available when we stop working. Simply put, we need to plan for our own retirement.

Why do we start here and not with investing for future special-needs expenses? Each of us will retire and live twenty to thirty years after retirement. For most, there is not a source of funds that will cover the basics needed during this time. Parents, caregivers, and guardians need to take care of themselves—financially, emotionally, and physically. A secure retirement gives you the resources needed to care for yourself and your family member with special needs.

There was a time when retirement income came from three sources: a company pension, Social Security benefits, and savings.

Company pensions started to disappear decades ago, and most workers today are not covered by a pension plan that guarantees them income in retirement. Teachers, those serving in the military, government workers, and some union employees are the main occupational groups that still have pensions.

Social Security benefits make up an important part of the average retiree's income. Social Security is a government system workers pay into until they reach a certain age. An individual can receive Social Security benefits at age sixty-two, but most people wait until sixty-six or sixty-seven so they can receive a higher monthly benefit.

Social Security is under stress, as there will be more people retiring over the next twenty years than there will be new workers to replace them and pay for the benefit. Changes are made from time to time to improve the system, but it looks like the younger generation will receive lower benefits than today's retirees. Social Security was not designed to replace all of the income you took home during your working years. It was there to supplement your own savings and pensions.

Pensions are gone. Social Security is questionable.

The third piece of the plan becomes the most important. You need to save for your retirement in accounts you control.

You will need to save at least 15 percent of your annual income over time to provide for yourself during your retirement years. The first part of Building Block 8 starts with this number: put 15 percent of your income to a retirement account.

Do not do more than this now. You have other goals to fund, including a special-needs trust and education accounts for other children. You can increase the amount you invest in your retirement accounts after you have these other investments in place.

SIMPLE RETIREMENT MATH

The math around retirement investing is simple—nothing more complicated that what you did in middle school. The average American family earns around $62,000 (according to 2009 census data). Fifteen percent of $62,000 is $9,300 per year, or $775 per month. That is the amount needed to fund retirement for the typical family.

This can be done. A typical American family spends that much on car loans, student loans, and credit cards each month. The average car payment for a used car in the United States is more than $350. For a new car it is closer to $500 per month. Eliminate the car payment, put it into a retirement account, and you have a healthy start on your savings. Take away other debt payments from credit cards and student loans, and you should have enough to fund your retirement account each year.

The simple math gets even better once you start investing. The US stock market has returned about 10 percent over long periods of time. A 10-percent return each year means your money will double every seven years. The $9,300 invested in a retirement account should double every seven years even if you do not add another dime to it. So the $9,300 invested the first year could double itself three times over if you have twenty-one years until retirement. A forty-four-year-old person today who puts $9,300 into an account this year and earns a 10 percent return will have $68,822 in a retirement account at age sixty-five—all without making any additional deposits during that time.

Amazing, right? Simple savings invested over time add up to real money.

Now, imagine saving that first $9,300 and adding another $9,300 to it each year. Over a period of twenty-one years, that $9,300 per year earns a total of more than $664,000. Add on a few extra years, and there will be almost a million dollars sitting in that account.

If you cannot invest 15 percent of your income in savings at first, start with a smaller amount. Do not wait until you have the full amount. Start at 3 percent, 6 percent, or whatever you can do right now. Put in $25, $50, or $200. Do not put so much away that you cannot pay your bills or risk starting the cycle of using credit again. But do something. Start now. Call human resources or a financial adviser today.

This is real money that will help carry you through retirement. This is real money that can be left to a special-needs trust if you do not use it all. Money in retirement accounts will generate income to use for living expenses, including money you can use for expenses related to your family member with special needs.

Investing takes time to pay off. It takes a decision today to put some money into savings and keep it invested throughout your working life. Income earned today is what will make you wealthy as long as you save 15 percent of it. This holds true if your family makes the average amount or a hundred times more than average.

Families should learn to live on their income, whatever that income is. It does seem easier to save and live if you earn $250,000 a year than $62,000. Unfortunately, the savings rate does not change much for families who earn more than average. Life becomes more expensive. Cars are more expensive, mortgage payments are higher, and clothes, dining bills, and other expenses creep up to meet the new income before an extra penny gets put into long-term investment accounts.

We have teachers, public school administrators, and military service people as clients. Each of the people in these fields chose heart over finances when entering the workforce. Enlisted personnel and teachers earn little during their first few years; many barely have enough to make ends meet. Most of the teachers I have met or worked with had two jobs for the first five or more years of work to afford a place to live and to feed a family. The people we meet in these fields have never earned $250,000. The last few years of a career in these fields may earn a teacher close to $75,000 and a colonel slightly more than $125,000. This is after years of average or below-average pay compared to the rest of the professional workforce.

Our clients who have a pension have more fulfilling retirements if they also saved in retirement accounts. Their pension provides for their basic needs, and their savings enables them to live their dream life. These families have found ways to save even though they had lower-than-average incomes for much of their careers. These are families who lived on what they earned and managed their finances around their take-home pay. They avoided getting into trouble with credit cards and home equity loans.

Successful families get used to spending less than they earn. Develop these habits today, and they will last you through retirement. Your spending behavior is crucial to success in retirement when you continue to spend only the amount you can afford.

Let investing math work in your favor. Put money to work at this point and begin moving your financial destiny toward wealth and security.

Why We Invest: Special-Needs Expenses

There is no simple rule of thumb for how much money to save for special-needs expenses, but there is some simple math. I find that people who have adult family members with developmental disabilities have a pretty good idea of how much extra they spend each month and year to support that person.

Here's a real-world example. A family I worked with had calculated the amounts they would need for future expenses each year. They expected to spend about $5,000 on medications, $5,000 on transportation, and another $10,000 per year for four years for additional education. The math here says that the person with special needs will need $10,000 per year during his lifetime plus another $40,000 for education expenses. The family knew they would likely pay for the education expenses during their working years, but they wanted to have enough to pay for the medications and transportation expenses for many years as well. Any family resource can be used for these expenses—saving accounts, retirement accounts, trusts, or retirement income.

Investing will help fund an account to pay for any future special-needs expenses. This way, you do not have to tap into your retirement funds.

Look at your budget to determine the expenses associated with your family member with special needs. Your financial planner can use these numbers to come up with the amount you need to save and invest to have funds available in the future.

At the very least, save 3 percent of your income in an investment account to fund a special-needs trust.

During retirement, expenses for family members with a disability do not go away. But how long will they last? My daughter with Down syndrome will likely live a long and healthy life. While her life expectancy is shorter than mine, there will be time when she is alive and I am not. She will need money to support her life regardless of whether I am still here.

I figure that my daughter with Down syndrome will need additional support for thirty years of life while I am retired, assuming I retire at sixty-five. She will also likely need support for another ten years after I am gone. My goal is to find a way to have enough money saved to spend on her needs during my retirement and then enough money for her to still receive money for ten years after my death.

WHY WE INVEST: EDUCATION FUNDS

College is a big expense that gets paid over a number of years. These expenses have a definite timeline to them. They start when a person finishes high school and last four years, per student. Of course, you need to account for additional years if your child plans on attending graduate school.

Every family handles this differently. Some want to pay for education; others want to contribute a set amount. Many others expect their children to work to pay for college. Have you decided what you plan to do?

Parents of newborns have eighteen years to save before the start of college. Those years pass quickly, and you want to invest as early as possible to help fund the cost of college. In-state tuition in Boulder, Colorado, costs about $26,000 per year. Four years of college at a state school right now costs about $100,000 across the country. Private colleges can cost up to $60,000 per year. These are big expenses.

The simple math of investing early decreases the amount you need to save to pay for college. One way to pay is to put some money in your savings account every year. If you put $5,000 a year into a savings account starting at your child's birth, you will have $90,000 saved for college (assuming your account earned no interest). That will pay for most of a state college expense in today's dollars. Unfortunately, inflation in college expenses has been high for decades, and that amount will not be enough.

The other option is to invest. We usually recommend investing inside a 529 plan for typical family members. At 7 percent per year, that $5,000 invested each year will be worth about $100,000 in twelve years. If you keep investing and your money keeps earning 7 percent, you will have about $187,000 in eighteen years. This gives your family member options on where to go and how to come out of college without a huge amount of debt.

INVESTING TOOLS, TOOLBOXES, AND WRAPPERS

I used to have a bright-red toolbox in my basement that my brother gave to me as a gift a long time ago. The gift was aspirational—I'm not the handiest person in the world. Still, over time, the toolbox was useful to hold my hammers, screwdrivers, nails, clamps, and the other tools I acquired. You just cannot own a home and not need some tools.

The toolbox not only held my tools, but it carried them as well. Each tool got used for a specific purpose; for example, a hammer got used to tap a nail into a piece of wood. The toolbox had one purpose, and each tool in turn had its own purpose.

People get confused about investing because there are so many terms out there. Stocks. Bonds. Mutual funds. Index funds. Exchange-traded funds. Annuities. Variable annuities. Indexed universal life. Individual retirement accounts. Roth IRAs. Managed futures. Hedge funds. 403(b)s.

HAVE I LOST YOU YET?

As you look at how to invest and which accounts to use, remember that there are tools and toolboxes. Here's a simple example that illustrates what I mean. An IRA is not an investment—it is a toolbox that holds investments. An IRA gives you tax advantages, the ability to choose beneficiaries, and potential income issues you must understand. Without the tools that it holds, the IRA does not do anything to help you build wealth.

Here's another example. A stock is not a toolbox—it is a tool. A stock can be owned in a number of different toolboxes. Trusts, IRAs, individual investment accounts, corporate entities, and your name on a piece of paper are all different toolboxes that can hold stocks.

Tools are your investments. They are assets. They are the parts of your financial life you expect to increase in value (or maintain value) over time. Basically, there are five tools used to invest: stocks, bonds, real estate, natural resources (commodities), or collectibles. Cash sitting in a money-market fund is a tool, but it is not an investing tool.

Some of your investments come in wrappers, or containers, just like some of the tools in my toolbox. I used to have a plastic box inside my toolbox with something like twenty compartments. This container held my screws, bolts, and washers. Even my wrenches had a separate plastic holder that sat in the toolbox. It's the same way with stocks, which are tools. They can be owned in a mutual fund, index fund, life insurance, or separate account, or they can be accessed through annuities. These wrappers can be expensive, like in an annuity, or relatively low in cost, like in a mutual fund or index fund. Most of these tools, regardless of whether they are in the wrapper, can be held in the different toolboxes.

Toolboxes enable you to own the five different types of investments. Retirement accounts are toolboxes. Trusts, brokerage accounts, or corporations are all types of toolboxes.

The wrappers may provide some benefits to just owning the tools. Mutual funds help diversify the number of stocks you own in one handy wrapper. They make it easier to hold and manage the underlying investments.

Toolboxes

Life would be easier if we could fit all our tools in one toolbox. As you invest, however, you need to use different kinds of toolboxes. This is not nearly as daunting as it seems. Make sure your advisory team helps you understand how using the different toolboxes in the right way can make a big difference in your life.

First Toolbox: The Savings Account

The first toolbox, the bank account, is easy to understand and simple to use; it's an insured bank account, a CD, or money-market funds. This toolbox holds emergency funds and any money you expect to use over the next twelve to thirty-six months. This toolbox does not hold anything complicated. Safety, security, and ease of access matter most for this toolbox.

Sometimes people look at this toolbox and see money just sitting there not doing much. Resist the temptation to take money from your bank account and put it into investments, retirement, or real estate. This toolbox is the first thing you reach for in times of stress. It needs to be easily accessible, stable, and usable without penalty.

This toolbox holds both emergency funds and escrow funds. You hold in this toolbox any money you expect to use for a significant life expense during the next three years.

Second Toolbox: The Retirement Account

The second toolbox you will use goes by the name "Retirement." It is often called by other names, such as 401(k), IRA, Roth IRA, 403(b), profit sharing plan, and others. Because of its different names and tax issues, this toolbox can be confusing.

People who have family members with special-needs should use the retirement toolbox with the word "Roth" in it. These are called Roth IRA, Roth 401(k), or are sometimes referred to as a post-tax retirement account.

Retirement Account Basics

This toolbox is complicated and needs some explanation. The retirement account toolbox was created within the tax code to encourage people to save for their retirement. Retirement accounts get several tax breaks from the government that increase their value for the people using them.

No taxes are paid on the money you invest in retirement accounts as that money accumulates. Some accounts, like Roth IRAs, have tax-free distributions as well. Savers who started young have ten, twenty, or thirty years to have tax-deferred or tax-free growth on their money in retirement accounts. This will add thousands or tens of thousands of additional funds that would otherwise go to taxes. The government is passing on tax revenue to encourage retirement savings—so take advantage of this benefit.

All retirement plans have government-mandated rules spelling out how and when you can get your money. Generally speaking, you cannot access the money you have in a retirement account until you are fifty-nine and a half without paying extreme penalties. That may seem restrictive, but the tax benefits for this trade-off are worth it.

Retirement accounts have rules allowing for access to funds without penalty in times of hardship, disability, education, and home ownership. Even here, you do not want to touch the retirement account. Followers of Blueprints have emergency funds to handle these situations, so the money in your retirement accounts can grow as long as possible.

Types of Retirement Accounts

Accounts fall into two tax types—pretax and post-tax funded. The difference has to do with when you get the tax benefit. These are usually called traditional (pretax) and Roth (post-tax).

Traditional (Pretax) Retirement Accounts. Traditional retirement accounts give the tax benefit during the tax year a contribution is made. The benefit happens now. The contribution lowers your current income and reduces your taxes the year you contribute.

Interest, dividends, and long-term capital gains are not taxed as they are earned over the years the money sits in the tax-deferred account. Taxes are paid when money comes out of traditional retirement accounts. My clients who have retired wish they did not have to pay taxes when they take the money from a traditional retirement account, but they enjoyed lower taxes while they worked.

Roth Accounts (Post-Tax Retirement Savings). These are usually the best types of retirement accounts for those who have a family member with special needs.

These types of families will focus their long-term retirement savings on Roth accounts. These can be a Roth IRA, Roth 401(k), or Roth 403(b). The tax treatment and rules governing a Roth make them great savings tools for families planning for their own retirement as well as funding future expenses for a person with special needs.

Contributions to a Roth account do not receive a current income-tax deduction. Money grows in a Roth account the same as any other retirement plan; income, dividends, and gains are not taxed. Investors have the same investment options in a Roth that they have in a traditional account. There is nothing different about the money in a Roth account versus traditional account while money grows and is invested for the future.

The big advantage of Roth accounts is when you take out the money.

You do not owe any taxes on the money you take out, no matter how much it has grown. You paid the taxes up front, set your tax liability with the government, and are now free to take out your money as you wish without having to think about what you still owe on it.

At death, no income tax is due to be paid by the beneficiary. This makes the Roth a far better tool than traditional accounts for most families, as all the money in the account can go to children or a special-needs trust.

Estate Planning and Income Taxes

Retirement accounts must be handled carefully for families who have members with special needs. Make sure your estate attorney and financial planner know about each retirement account you have. These retirement accounts should not be left to a person with special needs as the amount received will be a countable resource and could lead to a loss of benefits.

A traditional retirement account will owe income taxes the year the money comes out, no matter who gets it. If the money in the account is left to a trust, like a special-needs trust, then all the money in the account will count as income in the year distributed by the IRA.

I can't emphasize enough how important it is to consider the tax ramifications. If you do a great job saving, you could easily create $500,000 in your IRA to be used for retirement or to fund a trust. But look at what happens with a traditional account: The trust would recognize that $500,000 as income the year it is received. Most of the money will be taxed at the highest income tax rates—close to 45 percent of a mix of federal and state tax. In other words, if you haven't planned well, almost half of a traditional retirement account could be wiped out by taxes. The account could lose even more if you have to pay estate taxes.

A Roth account does not have the income tax issue when it is transferred to an estate. You paid the taxes while you worked. Let's say you have $500,000 in the account. That $500,000 transfers to the trust without any taxes due. A Roth lets you pass along the full amount in your retirement account to your special-needs trust without significant income tax complications. You can look at your account balance on your balance sheet each year and have a good idea of what you will leave to the trust from your Roth IRA.

Third Toolbox: Investment Accounts

Investment accounts do not provide any specific tax advantages. These accounts hold many of the same assets as retirement accounts, such as stocks, bonds, and mutual funds. These accounts allow you to invest for the long term and have access to funds without penalties when taking money out. These types of accounts can be used as a way to build assets that will go to the special-needs trust. We often use these for families who want to fund a special-needs trust.

The focus of this chapter is the three basic toolboxes most families with a member with special needs will have as they accumulate wealth: savings, retirement, and investment accounts. Two other types of toolboxes—trusts and education toolboxes—are also important. You should also be aware of a new toolbox, the Able Act account.

Fourth Toolbox: The Special-Needs Trust

Your estate plan creates this type of trust, which gets funded from investments sitting in the other types of toolboxes. The trust is a critical piece in following the Blueprints process so you can provide a high quality of life for your family member with special needs. Building Block 9 focuses on funding this type of trust.

Fifth Toolbox: Education Accounts

I do not recommend the use of 529 plans or any other education accounts for a person with special needs, as these accounts have the potential to cause a loss in benefits.

Funds for other children's college expenses should go into a 529 plan. These accounts allow for tax-free buildup of investments to be used for the expense of college and graduate school.

A 529 plan provides many of the same tax benefits of the Roth as long as money coming out of the plan is used for qualified education expenses. Qualified expenses include room and board, tuition, books, and more.

Most states sponsor 529 plans, but you do not have to use the one sponsored by your state; you can use the money in a 529 for college or graduate school expenses at any qualified institution in any state. Many states offer income-tax benefits to contributions. If your state has a highly rated plan and a decent income-tax benefit, use that one. If not, shop around for those with the best ratings.

Sixth Toolbox: Able Act Accounts

The Able Act was passed in 2015 and for the first time allows for people who qualify for SSI and other means-tested federal programs to have assets of more than $2,000 that they control. These accounts are similar to 529 plans: assets in the account grow tax free, and no taxes are paid on qualified disability expenses.

These qualified expenses must be for the benefit of the person and can include payments for such goods and services as employment training, medical equipment, housing, transportation, legal fees, wellness expenses, and more.

These accounts need to be treated with caution. Accounts with more than $100,000 can lead to a loss in SSI payments to the person with special needs. There are also some potential issues where a loss of benefits can occur if the distributions are not ones that benefit the person with special needs or can be turned into countable resources (like a large cash distribution).

The special-needs trust continues to play an important role in supporting those with special needs. Able Act accounts help give family members with special needs more independence and tax preference when handled the right way.

THE TOOLS OF THE TRADE: FIVE INVESTMENT OPTIONS

There are five main tools you can use for investments. The first two, stocks and bonds, are mostly common used for retirement funds. Stocks, bonds, and real estate are the most common tools used to fund a trust. We do not include cash or money market funds as an investment tool. These have a purpose in planning and are not long-term investments designed to increase in value.

If you have an investment portfolio and own a home, you likely own the first three tools. The other two tools—natural resources (commodities) and collectibles—are less commonly owned but can be an important part of your investments.

These five choices can be bought in many different types of toolboxes or in different types of wrappers. Mutual funds are the most common way for people to put their money to work. Don't confuse the way you buy your investments with what tool you are actually investing in.

Stocks

A stock represents an ownership interest in a company.

If you work in a small business, you know the owner. He comes in every day, sits near you, or walks around to see how you are doing. The local dry cleaner, garage repair shop, and plumbing company are likely owned by someone in your community. These people own their own companies. A "stock" is a piece of paper that represents an ownership share of a company. The dry cleaner owns 100 percent of that business and holds all the stock. Same with the plumber. There may be five people who own the local coffee shop, each having a share in the company.

Public companies, or those in the "stock market," sell shares to the general public. They have hundreds or thousands of owners, most of whom do not work at the company each day. Companies become public to raise money to grow and expand by selling shares. The stock (the shares of ownership) trades, and you can buy or sell shares of these companies.

Here's how it works: When you buy one share of Apple stock, for example, you now are a part owner in Apple. You and thousands of others make up the owners. Shareholders (owners) do not show up each day at Apple to run the business; they hire a CEO to run the company and a board of directors to help make good decisions on behalf of the shareholders.

Stocks earn money for owners in two different ways.

First, stocks may pay dividends. If Apple earns a profit, the people managing the business and shareholders may decide to pay a dividend to shareholders. In 2016, Apple paid $2.23 to each shareholder for each share owned. As companies earn more money, they may pay more dividends.

Second, stocks can appreciate in value. Stockholders have the chance to earn money when the value of the stock goes up. A company like Apple expects to earn money (be profitable) each year. If they make more than expected, there is a good chance the value of each share of stock will increase in value. These values change each day, month, and year as different stockholders decide to buy or sell shares depending on how they think Apple will do in the future. If they think Apple will earn less than expected, they could sell shares. If enough stockholders do this, the price will go down.

In 2016, most investors in Apple thought that profits would increase and that the shares would be more valuable. On the first trading day of 2016, the price of a share of Apple stock was $103.58. On December 31, 2016, a share of Apple stock sold for $115.82. Over that year, a stockholder earned $12.76 per share in appreciation.

Of course, the next month the price of a share could be higher or lower. Investing is a long-term exercise, and you do not want to get so caught up in the daily movements that you make poor investing decisions.

Bonds

Bonds represent money loaned to a government or business entity. You buy a single bond with a certain amount of money, such as $1,000. The company then pays interest on that bond each year (or several times per year). The bond earns income for you as the lender. The investor gets paid back the money at the end of a time period—for example, ten, twenty, or thirty years. Businesses use bonds to build new factories or expand operations. They expect to earn more than the cost of the interest rate and repayment amount over time.

Investors hold bonds to earn a regular, steady income and to have a high degree of security in their asset base. They are not seeking to grow wealth as they are with stocks. Bonds usually make up the more conservative part of your asset base.

Schools in many communities are built with bonds. A school may need to raise $5 million to build a new building and outfit classrooms with teaching materials and technology. They do this through a bond, where people in the community and other investors give $5 million to the school district. You may choose to buy $1,000 of that bond sale. The school district will pay back the $5 million to investors in a time period spelled out when they sell the bond— say twenty years. Each year, investors will receive a set percentage of income—something like 4 percent—an amount spelled out when the school district sells the bonds.

Let's say you decided to invest in this bond. Your $1,000 investment will earn $40 each year for the next twenty years. At the end of twenty years, you will receive the initial $1,000 back. Overall, the bond returned $800 in income in addition to your principal.

Bonds have several risks. The first is that you may not get paid back. This is called a default. The school district may have trouble collecting enough in taxes to pay the bond. Bonds have ratings to help guide investors on the risk of default.

Bonds also have an inflation risk. An interest rate of 4 percent looks good when banks pay less than 1 percent. But in the late 1970s and early 1980s, inflation increased dramatically, and some bonds paid 15 percent or higher. During such a period of high inflation, the 4 percent bond no longer looks very good. The purchasing power of your income goes down as inflation goes up.

Most people think bonds are less risky than stocks, and that has been true for the last few decades. It is one of the reasons people trade off the chance for the appreciation found in stocks for the income of bonds. People like bonds because of their predictable income stream and the high likelihood of getting money back at the end of a certain period of time.

Real Estate

Most of us know what real estate looks like—it is our house or apartment. Individuals usually own real estate in the form of a single-family home or condominium. Many Americans have significant net worth in homes.

Others choose to invest in real estate as a way to increase income and build assets. If you rent, someone owns your building—and that person or company has decided to invest in real estate. You may decide to do this as well.

Investors can own real estate by buying single-family homes, apartment properties, or office space to rent to others. Individual real estate investors like single-family homes or small rental buildings because they can improve those properties with their hard work, something called "sweat equity." Painting, new landscaping, and other simple fixes often increase the value of the property. The income can be predictable if the building or apartments are rented out.

But real estate has some downsides. Vacancies can turn an income property into a money pit. Maintenance must be done and tenant interests responded to quickly. Too many investors get into debt on rental properties and then run into trouble as they do not have the cash needed for maintenance or to pay the lender when there are vacancies.

Real estate can also be difficult to sell during downturns in the market, so you need to be able to hold your real estate through these times to recover your basic investment.

Real estate can be bought through the public market and can provide the high degree of liquidity and marketability many families want. This is done through real estate investment trusts (typically referred to as REITs). REITs offer many of the advantages of owning your own real estate without the management headache. Historically, REITs pay higher income than stocks in other companies. They are required by tax laws to pass through the majority of income to their owners each year. REITS, like stocks, are priced during trading hours and can be bought or sold easily.

Natural Resources (Commodities)

Commodities are things like oil, natural gas, gold, copper, and corn. The last decade has seen an explosion in demand from investors trying to enrich themselves from the earth's bounty and through investment vehicles designed to help make that happen.

Research over the past twenty years seemed to show that having a part of your investments in natural resources helped add additional return without too much extra risk if these holdings were kept to a small percentage of your portfolio. Part of this return may have come from demand created by economic expansion in China, and part from the fact that people all around the world have an ever-increasing need for energy to power homes and cars. Demand for food continues to increase as people move from living in poverty to enjoying a middle-class lifestyle. Building materials like lumber, copper, and more are needed as new homes are built in a modern way throughout the world.

In the past, investing in natural resources required investors to have large dollar amounts to invest through futures contracts. Today, mutual funds and exchange-traded funds allow small and large investors alike to put money toward natural resources in highly liquid, quickly traded securities.

Natural resources do have significant risks associated with them that are different from the risks associated with stocks, bonds, and REITS. They do not pay current income, so investors cannot earn money while waiting for values to rise. Natural resources are also at risk of world events—for example, conflict in the Middle East drives oil prices higher, and the end of a conflict leads to a quick drop in price. Timing can make a big difference on your earnings potential with natural resources.

Collectibles

Some of my clients have interests in life that mesh with their investing goals—and they wish to buy something related to their interests, hobbies, and passions. At times, these purchases gain in value like other investments. Other times, they stay in a family to be appreciated for their intrinsic beauty, historical value, or utility, not for any monetary gain. These items fall into the category of collectibles.

Collectibles range from precious artwork—like a Picasso painting—to a vintage car sitting in a garage waiting to be fixed. Beanie Babies, sculptures from local artists, antique furniture, ceramic figurines, coins, baseball cards, and other physical objects are examples of other things that fall into the category of collectibles. One of my clients owned three classic violins, including a Stradivarius. These violins were investments that also brought great joy to the owner and others when played.

Some collectibles, like classic works of art and rare coins, usually increase in value over time. They require special handling, insurance, and security to maintain that value. Others, like Beanie Babies, may seem like an investment when the entire world wants them, but they end up being nothing more than a fad that does not hold value.

It can be difficult to tell which collectibles will maintain value and which will not. New artists without a proven track record could be widely collected initially, but their art can quickly disappear without anyone wanting to buy it. Antiques from a certain historical period change in value with fashion, and the value of these pieces changes with the times.

Owners of collectibles get to enjoy and appreciate their investments each day. The art on walls, the cars in garages, or the coins in collections can be viewed, held, used, and used as part of everyday life. This does not happen with a stock or a bond.

No public market exists for collectibles. Often collectibles must be sold in private transactions or auctions where prices are determined between buyer and seller. An expert in coins will have an advantage over the collector who just starts out.

The margins are high in collectibles; the price paid includes a significant amount of money going to the broker. Taxes on gains in collectibles are higher than long-term gains on stocks and bonds, so make sure you understand the tax impact if you get involved here.

These types of investments should not be used when you need income from your investments or have a particular deadline by which you need to access your asset values. The market for your collection may be down when you need and want to sell. It is harder to count on a collectible for long-term spending needs than on your other investments.

LIQUIDITY AND MARKETABILITY

What would you do if you had to raise money tomorrow for an emergency medical treatment? Or what if you want to buy a car next month? How do you expect to pay for the family vacation next year?

Would you just sell your house? Take your coin collection down to the dealer and hope for the best? No, you need to have accessible funds.

As you think about your investments, make sure you understand how liquid and marketable your investments are. Liquid means they can be easily turned into cash. Marketable means there are many buyers and sellers for your investment.

In Blueprints, we recommend families have significant portions of their investments in stocks and bonds that can be quickly turned into cash or can generate cash dividends (these may be in mutual funds or other types of toolboxes). The money you need for income or for big purchases cannot be tied up in assets that are hard to sell or take a long time to sell.

Stocks, bonds, REITs, and certain kinds of natural-resource holdings can be held in publicly traded securities that are highly liquid and marketable. The prices can be seen at any time of the day. For example, a share of IBM stock can be sold any day the stock market is open. Millions of shares of IBM are traded each day, so there is a ready market for people who want to buy or sell. One share will not change the price much, so you can pretty much know what you will get for your share of IBM at the time you decide to sell it. IBM stock is both marketable (turned into cash at close to its current price) and liquid (meaning able to be sold quickly).

Real estate, gold, private businesses, and artwork, on the other hand, are examples of investments that are not liquid. They take time and effort to sell. A rental property could take days, weeks, or even a year or more to sell at a price you want. In fact, it might never sell at the price you want or think it is worth. A gold coin requires time to get prices from dealers, and that price can vary widely depending on the dealer and the current demand for that particular type of coin.

Most people should have most of their money in highly liquid and marketable investments. Other investment options can work and could represent a piece of your net worth, but not until you reach the time where your balance sheet is stable, your emergency funds are in place, and your highly marketable and liquid investment accounts contain enough to provide security.

MUTUAL FUNDS—YOUR PRIMARY INVESTMENT WRAPPER

Every portfolio should start with mutual funds. In fact, most of your money should be in mutual funds throughout your investing life. Investors with higher net worth will likely add individual stocks and bonds to a portfolio, but mutual funds are the starting place. These are important wrappers for the investing tools.

Investors can buy shares of companies, such as IBM, Coca-Cola, or Apple. These investments in individual companies can work great if you pick the right company at the right time and hold it long enough. Most individual investors do not do this. They do not want to review global economic news or accounting figures or research individual companies.

The biggest risk in owning stock in an individual company is that the company can change dramatically for the worse. Companies can and do go out of business. Enron, WorldCom, and others are examples of companies where stock investors lost everything. Most investors do not own enough stocks in companies to spread out the risk in case one company fails or does poorly.

On the other hand, a mutual fund combines the money of hundreds of thousands of people. In this case, you give your money to a mutual fund company, and the managers of that fund invest it for you. The managers are investment companies and investment professionals who buy and sell the investments on your behalf.

Mutual funds reduce risk by owning dozens or hundreds of companies. A fund may have a few lousy companies, but it will also have plenty that are excellent. Mutual funds give investors diversification.

These fund companies send a statement each month or report your values to your brokerage firm each day. And mutual funds can be bought or sold every day, giving you access to your money as needed.

A mutual fund does not mean a particular kind of investment type. Some invest in dividend-paying stocks, others in government bonds. Some mutual funds invest in companies in Europe, others in global technology. Investors choose the type of fund based on objectives, time horizons, and other factors.

There are two types of mutual funds—actively managed funds and index funds. Actively managed funds are those that have a team of people working to decide on which stocks or bonds (or other tools) to own in the fund. They use economic research, industry trends, profit and loss statements, interviews with CEOs, cost/benefit determinations, and a huge number of other factors to decide when to buy or sell a stock, bond, or other security.

Index funds use a formula to determine how to invest the money. Their managers buy and sell investments to track the formula. You have heard the names of these formulas in the news. The S&P 500 and the Dow Jones Industrial Average (the Dow) are the most common. The Nasdaq is another. So is the US Aggregate Bond Index (the Agg). The S&P 500 contains the five hundred largest publicly traded companies in the United States as determined by a research firm started by a company called Standard and Poor's (S&P). There is no magic to the S&P 500, but it does do a great job of representing the leading companies in the United States. The Dow has thirty companies in it, and the team who creates the list seeks to have a basket of companies representing key industries and the key players in those industries.

A great debate and never-ending argument exists between the use of active management and index funds for investors. The portfolios I manage usually have a mix of index and actively managed funds, as I think they complement each other. Your adviser will have a preference. There will not be much difference over time between broad-based index funds or active funds investing in similar areas if your active funds have a solid, long-term track record and the management team and guiding philosophy stays the same throughout market cycles.

Ask your investment adviser how she chooses funds. You do not need to pick your own funds, but you do need to know the thinking and philosophy behind how your adviser works and makes selections and recommendations for you.

THREE DRIVERS OF INVESTMENT SUCCESS

New investors should be familiar with a few investment concepts that drive how most people invest over time. These are not technical details of how to rate a fund, pick a stock, or develop a trading strategy. These are the big ideas that drive how many financial planners and "target-date" funds in your retirement plan work.

The three most important terms in investing are *asset allocation*, *rebalance*, and *review*. The first two terms refer to investment philosophy; the third refers to checking your progress every few years and assessing your life situation to make sure you're on track in accomplishing your goals.

Asset Allocation

You should have money in different types of investments—some in a money market (cash balances), some in US stocks, some in international stocks, and some in bonds. *Asset allocation* is the process of taking different investment options and deciding how much to put in each.

Financial planners use stocks, bonds, and money market funds (cash) as the three primary asset classes when building portfolios. Real estate, commodities, private businesses, and collectibles need to be included in the discussion as well if you decide to invest in those asset classes.

Most financial planners rely on the concepts of asset allocation to design portfolios and make assumptions about your long-term investment returns. US stocks have provided investors with returns between 10 and 12 percent over long periods of time. These are the average returns you got in the past if you stayed invested for decades. Most planners assume you will get something similar in the future even as the market moves up and down in any given month or year.

An investment portfolio must fit your needs. There is no one right allocation for every investor. The first two investment tools—stocks and bonds—are where you will have most of your money. These tools have the most people investing in them, have established track records, and have been used by millions of people and thousands of institutions to create wealth.

Stocks and bonds are also the best understood of the asset classes. We have a pretty good idea of how they have responded to both good economic news and bad economic news. Stocks and bonds have been studied throughout all kinds of economic situations and periods of global strife, including the Great Depression, World Wars I and II, Vietnam, the Great Recession, the tech bubble, and all the boom periods in between and around those events.

Your allocation to each asset class is considered the largest factor in whether your portfolio grows quickly or slowly in good times and how much it can decrease in value through difficult times. The more you hold in cash and bonds, the less chance you have for your portfolio to increase in value over time. The more you have in stocks, the more you have a chance to make money.

The biggest challenge investors face is keeping their asset allocation strategy in place throughout market cycles. Asset allocations need to be made based on life events, planning needs, and current assets—not on emotions around making or losing money in investments. Unfortunately, individual investors have a lousy track record. They tend to jump out of their investments when the investment returns are at their lowest and jump back in when values peak. Study after study shows individual investor returns average just under inflation when stock mutual funds average between 10 and 12 percent over time. Individual investors acting on their own do not make good decisions about the markets.

Asset allocation represents one type of diversification. Through asset allocation, you have some money in money-market funds, some in bonds, and some in stocks (both in the US and internationally). There are times when stocks do well and bonds do not. There are times when bonds do well and stocks do not. Owning both asset classes gives you a chance to have one do well to support your portfolio even if the other does not.

You will need to have broad diversification within each asset class as well. You do not want all your stocks in five or ten companies or in the same type of company; for example, you don't want too much in technology stocks and none in oil and gas. The economy does not impact each type of company at the same time. One sector, like energy, may be having a lousy year at a time when transportation companies are doing well.

Companies can and do fail. By owning dozens (or more) of stocks and dozens (or more) of bonds, you help protect yourself from the risk being invested in only one or two that suddenly develop catastrophic problems.

Rebalance

Rebalancing is the process of keeping the target asset allocation in place. In some years, stocks do extremely well; in other years, bonds do better than stocks. Your target allocation today may be something like 55 percent in US stocks, 20 percent in international stocks, and 25 percent in bonds. If the stock market has a few great years in a row, you could wind up with 80 or 90 percent in stocks pretty quickly—something that would be considered a more aggressive portfolio. You need to adjust your portfolio at least once a year to get it close to the target allocation of your financial plan. That process is called rebalancing.

Investors fall in love with the parts of the portfolio that work best. In early 2009, it was hard to get investors to take money from bonds and put it toward stocks. They had just lived through historic market turmoil and were nervous. Stocks tumbled. Bonds did incredibly well. Not many people wanted to sell bonds in the early part of 2009 to buy stocks. Those who did seemed like gamblers. Looking back, those who rebalanced at this time made back losses far faster than the average investor. The act of rebalancing on a regular schedule forces you to make investment decisions based on sound theories rather than on market emotions.

The same held true during the end of the tech bubble. Many investors had too much in stocks, and too many of those stocks were in technology. Those who rebalanced across their industries did not suffer the huge losses tech investors did.

Rebalancing protects you against having a long-term investment profile that does not suit your needs. You could end up too conservative or too aggressive, depending on market moves. Rebalancing at least once a year forces you to make good investment decisions.

Review

Your financial life changes over time. A detailed financial plan provides a way to update and understand how your asset allocation is helping you achieve your goals. The plan can tell if you are on track based on savings, investment returns, debt, age, and goals. Two forty-year-olds who earn the same amount of money will have different portfolios depending on what they wish to do in life and how much they save. Families with special needs will have to save more or invest for growth longer than typical families.

You will see a shift in your attitude and excitement about investing after you pay off your debts. You do not have to worry about each and every market fluctuation when you have the peace of mind and financial security that comes with following the Blueprints process. Those in debt look at each change in market values each month and think about money they could have used to pay toward debts. Those with no payments look at how their money grows each month as those payments are put to work to grow wealth.

The review lets you know if you are on track and what adjustments can and should be made to stay on track as easily as possible. You will adjust your asset allocation to become more aggressive or conservative depending on your financial plan and need to continue to invest.

VALUE AN INVESTMENT ADVISER AND FINANCIAL PLANNER

The right investment adviser is a partner who can help you make the best investment decisions and who can connect you to leading attorneys, accountants, and other members of your professional team.

Leading advisers add value to your investment portfolio. They screen the world of mutual funds and other investments to help you choose the best ones to suit your needs. They manage the process of choosing an asset-allocation strategy, rebalancing portfolios, and reviewing your entire financial situation. They implement your investment strategy and handle all the details.

Today, many advisers recognize their fiduciary obligation to clients. This means that your interests come before those of the adviser or her firm. The big companies and insurance companies have fought to be covered under the fiduciary standard. Seek an adviser who will look after your interests first. Most of these advisers prefer to work on a fee basis.

Unfortunately, financial advice is littered with people who do not have your best interests in mind. They sell products that do not take into account your specific needs. They get paid on a transaction basis, so they don't have an incentive to work with you over time. They have one or two products to fit every situation—they sell a hammer, and all they see are nails.

You want a financial adviser who is not affiliated with an insurance company and ideally is with an independent financial firm that has been in practice for at least five years. This person needs to be a Certified Financial Planner professional (CFP).

Interview several financial planners and ask each the same questions. This will give you a good idea of how they work, who they are as people, and how they can help you. Do not be intimidated into making a decision at the first meeting. You will work with your financial planner for many years. Personal connection is important, and you need to make sure your planner has the right skills, abilities, and mindset to be of service to your family.

The following are some sample questions you should ask a potential financial planner:

1. Describe a typical client. How many clients do you have?
2. What are your credentials and educational background?
3. Have long have you been an adviser? How long has your firm been in business?
4. What makes you a good adviser?
5. What types of clients do you have?
6. Do you or your firm have any current or prior disciplinary issues?
7. Do you have a client specialty?
8. What services do you offer, and which do you most use with clients?
9. Do your clients get a written plan? Is there an additional cost?
10. How often will you communicate with me?
11. What is your experience working with families like mine?
12. How do you charge?
13. Do you use models or platforms or provide individualized portfolios?

 Worksheet: Choosing a Financial Planner

Take time at home to review the conversations from the meeting, and do not feel pressured to make a decision in the adviser's office. After meeting with an adviser, ask yourself some additional questions: Is this adviser sales oriented or education oriented? Does this person have my best interests at heart, and does he or she have the professional ability to help me? The answers to these questions will help you make a wise decision about a professional with whom you will work for a long time in helping meet your important goals and dreams.

BUILDING WEALTH

You are now on track to build the assets you need to retire comfortably, pay for future special-needs expenses, cover education expenses, enjoy the dreams on your bucket list, and give to charities.

The hardest steps are now behind you, and you get to enjoy the work you have done. Retirement accounts and investment accounts will grow faster than you could have imagined as those payments you made to lenders now are saved and invested for yourself. The Blueprint of your dreams starts coming into reality each and every month you save money in the accounts that can earn money for you.

BUILDING BLOCK 9

Funding the Trust

The last Building Block in Blueprints helps you choose assets to fund a special-needs trust. Blueprints has already showed you how to put the trust in place, get out of debt, create emergency funds, and begin to save for your own retirement. Now you will start funding the trust you have established.

The steps you take here will make the difference between your family member living in poverty and living a high quality of life. This Building Block adds color, joy, and freedom of choice to the life of your family member with a disability by having money available to benefit that person.

Government programs—like Medicaid and Supplemental Security Income—are not designed to create a fabulous, exciting, and fulfilling life for anyone. These programs provide basic support so a person with special needs has some food and a place to live.

Families who have members with special needs must create assets to be used for any other future expenses. Jobs for people with developmental disabilities are not plentiful and do not pay well. It is up to us to provide for them—now and in the future. Parents and other family members must make up the difference between a life of bare existence and a life full of activity, entertainment, and richness by investing funds for the future.

LONGER LIVES

Decades ago, the life expectancy of people with special needs was far shorter than it is today. For example, according to the National Down Syndrome Society, in 1983 the average person with Down syndrome was expected to live until age twenty-five; today, the average life expectancy is sixty. Changes to care, health, nutrition, and attitude all have made a tremendous difference in the lives of our family members with special needs.

My daughter was born with heart and thyroid issues, both of which are fairly common in people with Down syndrome. Her first cardiologist told me that not too long ago the medical community did not think it worthwhile to fix the heart of an infant with Down syndrome. Part of this had to do with medical abilities, and part of it had to do with how little the medical community valued a person with special needs. Today, success rates for this type of surgery are high. People with special needs no longer are denied medical procedures that can help them live long and healthy lives.

Today, my daughter no longer has a heart issue; her cardiologist considers her to have a typical heart. She is not limited in her activities as a result of a heart condition that would have prevented her from being as fit, active, and healthy as she is today.

What about my daughter's thyroid condition? The thyroid is critical in helping children develop overall health and improved brain function. Thyroid medication has been inexpensive and available for a long time, yet decades ago it was often not prescribed for people with Down syndrome. Without a simple and inexpensive drug, my daughter would not have had the chance to reach her current abilities in reading, social activities, and school.

These two changes to medical care and the attitudes surrounding it will result in a much longer life expectancy for my daughter. She will live a long, healthy, happy life.

My daughter will likely outlive me. I turned thirty-seven years old seven weeks before her birth. If I live to be eighty-seven—a likely thing today—she will be fifty when I pass away. On average with today's advances, she will live at least ten more years—and that span could continue to increase with new medical advancements. My planning needs to include finding a way to pay for her additional expenses through my work years, during my retirement, and after I am gone.

In other words, I need to find a way to leave money to a trust—enough money to cover the things I want her to have when I am not here.

In the past, families with a member with special needs did not plan to leave a legacy to support that person. Today, every family needs to review their expectations for saving and investing to be able to continue the quality of life provided today well into the future.

Many families I meet do have loved ones with special needs who are medically fragile and are not expected to outlive their parents. No matter what, you need to take action and put a special-needs trust in place just in case you pass away earlier than expected. This chapter talks about funding the trust. All families who have a member with special needs need to have a special-needs trust in place as the foundation for the rest of their planning work.

This chapter will show you ways to fund the trust, whether you pass away unexpectedly in the near-term or many years from now.

DIFFERENT PLANNING PHASES

Funding the trust looks different depending on how far along you are in the Blueprints process.

The focus at the beginning is to determine your goals, get your estate plan with special-needs provisions in place, eliminate debt, build an emergency fund, and save for retirement.

As you get your financial house in order, you will start making new decisions about how to fund a trust and how much you wish to direct to that trust. With the basic Building Blocks in place, you are beginning to build assets. You know your retirement is in good shape, as you are putting 15 percent into your retirement accounts. You may have decided to fund education accounts for your other children.

Now you want to build assets to give to the trust in the future. This step includes working with your financial planner to determine how much money you want to leave to the trust and which assets will fund the trust when you pass away.

This section assumes your transfers to a trust will happen in the future, when you or another family member pass away. In most cases, you do not want to give assets to a trust while you are alive.

AN EMPTY BUCKET

Trusts get set up in one of two ways.

One is through the will and probate process. Many people have the trust set up through the will, to be paid at the time of death. The trust does not sit there today; it springs into being later. Initially, this is how I had my special-needs trust set up. The attorney handling my estate set up the trust to hold the assets for my daughter with special needs at the time of my death as part of my will.

Later, I changed this. I set up a trust with its own tax identification number. This is a trust available to hold funds at any time.

Why did I change this? One family member wanted to help and indicated her desire to give my daughter money through her own estate plan. To do this, she needed to point her own estate plan toward a trust for my daughter. Otherwise, she would have had to send money directly to my daughter—and, as you know, that would have ruined all the work and planning we had done by making my daughter ineligible for important government help.

Most of the time, the trust gets funded only when someone passes away. Special-needs trusts are not like bank, investment, or retirement accounts. There is no simple way to make contributions to the trust account without complicated tax filings. Think of your trust as an empty bucket while you are alive. The bucket is there to hold assets at the right time but remains empty until then.

Too often people fund trusts without understanding the tax and legal issues involved that can impact the ability of their family member to stay on benefits. But thanks to what you've learned throughout the Blueprints process, you know that the special-needs trust should not have anything in it—no money market funds, life insurance, or any other assets.

Some special-needs trusts acquire money sooner. These are first-party (my own money for my benefit) special-needs trusts. These must be done with an attorney and approved by your state Medicaid representative office. They are different from the planning work covered in Blueprints.

THREE PARTS OF THE BUILDING BLOCK

You need to determine three key things in funding a special-needs trust:

1. How much will I leave to each family member?
2. How do I decide how much I want to leave to the special-needs trust?
3. Which assets should I use to fund the trust?

1. Dividing Your Estate

Building Block 4 helps you understand why a special-needs trust is so important. You need that trust in place to make sure you protect available government benefits for your family member. You will waste precious family resources if you do not have a special-needs trust.

Each family must decide who will be included in any estate plan. Some families choose to divide their assets equally. Others give more to the family member with special needs through the trust. There is no right answer. You have to make a decision that works for your family.

As children grow up, it is easier to understand the needs, costs, and abilities of each heir and who will need more or less as part of your estate plan. Some families calculate the future need of their family member and aim to fund a trust with that amount; they then leave the rest to the other heirs.

2. Determining the Amount of the Special-Needs Trust

There are two ways to determine how to fund your special-needs trust.

Some families do not really know how much they will need in the future. It is difficult to tell whether a four-year-old person with autism will be able to work as an adult. Many families prefer to start with a monthly dollar amount to save and invest for the future of their family member with special needs.

Start by putting at least 3 percent of your income away for the trust. Invest that money in mutual funds in an investment account. By this point, you have started saving 15 percent of your income to a Roth retirement account (or a traditional retirement account if that is what is offered by your employer). Now, take an additional 3 percent of your pay and put it into an investment account with your financial planner in an account in your name. This first method works in the short term.

The second method works better over the long term for your family. Highlight the expenses on your budget that you pay for your family member. These will fall into a few general categories:

Basic living. This section includes extra money you pay for items not paid by SSI and Medicaid to support your family member. Food and housing costs are not allowable expenses to be paid by a trust if a person is covered by SSI. Review your other line-item expenses for your family member such as clothing, medical care, and costs for basic living and health.

Quality of life. These items include cable, subscriptions, entertainment, travel, and anything else you pay for to make life enriching, exciting, and fulfilling for your family member with special needs. Look at what else you pay for to support your family member with special needs; what have you paid for on a regular basis during the last twelve to twenty-four months? Your budget will show you know how much you spent on dining out, movies, coffee, and life's big and little pleasures.

Transportation. Consider what you pay for taxis, gas, bus fares, other modes of transportation, and any out-of-pocket expenses related to your family member with special needs. Will she need to pay for transportation to get to work, engage in the community, or get to social events?

Future goals. Look back at your work in Building Block 1 and see what else you need and want to plan for to provide the best possible life for your family member with special needs. Does this include a condo in which she can live independently? Will you want to pay for new medical equipment and therapies in the future that you do not pay for now? Here you will have to estimate costs for some of the goals on your list. Do this based on what these things would cost today. A condo in your area may cost $100,000; use that figure instead of trying to guess what a condo will cost fifteen or thirty years from now.

Adding It Up to Fund the Trust

Once you have reviewed your budget for payments to support your family member with special needs, list them below or on the worksheet. Use an annual amount here; if you've figured what monthly expenses are, multiply the monthly number by twelve.

Basic Living   _____
Quality of Life   _____
Transportation   _____
Future Goals   _____

 Worksheet: Funding a Trust

Next, estimate how long that money will be needed to support your family member. Take a guess at how long this will be. People with some disabilities have almost the same life expectancy as the rest of the population; others are expected to live for a much shorter period of time.

Number of years _____

Multiply your expense number per year by the number of years you expect to need money in the trust.

Amount needed for trust _____

You now have a working goal for how much money to get into the trust. This figure represents what it costs today to pay for future expenses.

This is not the amount you have to leave to the trust.

There are several other factors to consider when deciding how much money you should leave for the trust. This is where you need a good financial planner.

Assets in the trust will earn money over time. Building Block 7 gives you investment basics. The assets in the trust will earn dividends and grow if invested in a mix of stocks and bonds. Discount the amount of money needed to fund the trust by how much you expect your investment returns to be. Generally, we use more conservative estimates in a special-needs trust than for retirement and other long-term goals.

You need to factor inflation into the amount you leave in a trust. Nothing costs the same today as it did ten years ago, and medical costs increase faster than the cost of basic food and shelter. Your trust assets need to grow by at least the rate of inflation over time to keep purchasing power the same as it is today. We talk about future expenses in today's dollars, and our inflation adjustment helps keep that money growing to be able to buy those goods and services in the future.

Your financial planner will help you take your budget number and create a savings and investment plan designed to fund your trust.

Creating Assets to Fund the Trust

Unfortunately, there are no good tax-sheltered ways to save for your family member with special needs. Your Roth IRA will be needed for retirement. Congress did pass the Able Act account legislation, but this does not help families save enough to fund a trust to cover expenses for a lifetime. Able Act accounts are best used as an account for your family member with special needs to use to have greater independence on her own spending.

Your best option is an investment account. Take the 3 percent of income or any other amount you can save for the future and put it into an investment account. This account can have income-generating pieces if you will need the money soon and growth pieces for the longer term. Investment accounts give you the liquidity and access to funds you may need for your family member with special needs.

The next step is to designate which of your other assets will go to the trust. When someone dies, they will likely have money left in savings, checking, investments, and retirement accounts. They may own a home, car, and other assets. They may also have investments in real estate or businesses. Work with a financial planner to help you understand how much you may have left in your estate. Many of our clients expect to have money left over in retirement accounts to pass along to the next generation.

3. *Designate Assets to the Trust*

Do not simply divide each of your assets equally to your beneficiaries—some assets are better used than others for a trust.

By now you have assets in three or four categories: savings accounts, retirement accounts, in real estate (if you own a home), and possibly in an investment account. You may also have life insurance, annuities, and other assets.

Each type of asset has unique tax rules, liquidity, and the ability to be used in the short term. Savings accounts are pretty simple: $15,000 sitting in the bank can be easily transferred to the trust through the probate process. No income taxes will need to be paid. The trust now has $15,000 to be used all at once or in small amounts over time; however, the trustee determines what is best.

Other assets do not transfer as easily. Income taxes will need to be paid on traditional retirement accounts if they are moved to a special-needs trust. Investment assets moved into a trust before death may require that capital gains taxes be paid. Homes designated to fund a special-needs trust will encounter costs of transferring, maintaining, and keeping the home over time.

As you follow the Building Blocks, you should have no debt (except maybe a mortgage), money in emergency funds, additional savings for short-term needs, and investment accounts you are using to build wealth. You should also have a Roth IRA or Roth 401(k). These are the simplest assets to leave to anyone in an inheritance. The money in these types of accounts is easy to transfer, easy to determine the value of, and easy to understand by trustees and family members.

The following section will help you understand which of your assets to use to fund a trust today and how to create assets to fund a trust in the future.

THE BIG THREE

Savings accounts, investment accounts, and Roth accounts are the best types of assets to use to fund a special-needs trust. None have special tax issues. None have ongoing maintenance costs. They are simple to move (unlike a house, business, or collection of art). The trustee can quickly use the assets in these three kinds of accounts to benefit your family member without any headaches or worries.

Other assets and account types are useful, of course, but they take longer or have other complications to work out before they can be used. You want the trustee to be able to act quickly to benefit your family member.

Savings Accounts

Savings and other bank accounts have a certain value on your date of death. The money in these accounts simply transfers to the special-needs trust or to the other beneficiary you designate in your will. Your $20,000 emergency fund now becomes a trust asset or belongs to another family member.

Investment Accounts

Investment accounts also transfer easily to a trust or heir. There are no income-tax issues on these accounts, as the heirs receive the investment holdings at the value they show at the date of death.

Many families now choose to have bank accounts and investment accounts transferred through a beneficiary designation rather than a will. Financial institutions use a simple form to help you set up a POD ("payable on death") or TOD ("transfer on death") on these accounts. Assets with these designations do not go through the will and probate; they are directed to the beneficiaries you determine when you sign the form. This makes clear who gets which assets.

Be careful with these forms. Only fill them out after talking with your estate attorney. You could make your planning worse by using these forms the wrong way.

One client came to me as a result of the poor use of a TOD. She had a sister with special needs, and her mother had taken steps to leave a portion of her estate to the special-needs trust. Somewhere along the way, Mom moved her investment accounts to an adviser who was not familiar with special-needs issues. The adviser recommended using a TOD to transfer assets to each adult child in equal shares.

Bad idea.

Mom died, and a portion of the investment account went to the daughter with developmental disabilities in her own name. The TOD on the account meant the trust did not get a share of the account; the person with special needs did. It was a disaster. The family scrambled to spend down some of the money inherited by the sister with special needs and to get a new trust set up that would allow her to resume getting her federal benefits. During that time, they feared losing her benefits and worried about the significant changes it would have meant for everyone involved.

The TOD should have pointed the share of the family member with special needs to her trust, and everything would have worked fine. The mother would have been better off not using the designation on the account and letting the personal representative of the estate handle everything.

Roth IRAs and Roth 401(k)

Roth accounts are also great ways to leave money to a special-needs trust. These assets transfer to a beneficiary and to a trust without having to pay any income or growth taxes when the transfer is made. The money in a Roth accounts has had the chance to grow tax free the entire time it has been in the account, and there are no income taxes or penalties to pay to a trust beneficiary.

It's critical to remember that the Roth cannot go directly to the person with special needs. The beneficiary of the Roth must be the trust or another family member. Like any other type of account, a Roth owned by a person with special needs will count as a resource and could cause that person to lose their SSI and Medicaid benefits. Money going to the trust will have to lose the tax-free status of the Roth IRA, which is fine. The account has had years of tax-free growth. Now it must go to the trust.

The personal representative and trustee will work together to have any Roth accounts transferred to a trust.

OTHER OPTIONS

Traditional Retirement Plans

Traditional IRAs, 401(k)s, and other retirement accounts can also be used to fund a trust. Traditional retirement accounts have tax issues that make them less useful when passing assets to a special-needs trust than do savings, investment, and Roth accounts.

Traditional retirement accounts give you a tax break: your current income is reduced, and you do not pay income taxes on the money you put into the account the year you contribute. The money grows in the account without you having to pay any taxes as long as no distributions are taken. This works great for people earning more during their working years than they expect to earn during retirement, as they should be in a lower tax bracket and pay lower effective taxes during retirement.

However, this does not work well for passing along money to heirs in special-needs trusts. To fund a trust, the money must come out of the IRA as a distribution after the owner of the IRA dies. When the money is transferred, it becomes taxable. No income taxes have been paid until this point. The trust will owe taxes on the amount transferred from the account—and taxes will be due for the full amount left to the trust at rates of 20 percent, 30 percent, or more. In some states, close to another 10 percent will be due in state income taxes.

In all, 45 percent or more of the balance in a traditional IRA could go to pay income taxes.

If amounts are high enough, there may also be estate taxes due.

This tax bite should be carefully considered when using a traditional retirement account as a cornerstone of your savings plan for the special-needs trust. Use a Roth instead to reduce this long-term tax hit to your trust plan.

Traditional retirement accounts may be better left to other family heirs. You can leave your traditional retirement account to other family members, and they have the ability to take the tax hit over time if you name individuals as beneficiaries. They can stretch the tax bite over their lifetime and keep the tax advantages of the traditional account in a way that a trust beneficiary cannot.

Review which retirement account types you are using. Start a Roth to use the tax code to your advantage to fund the trust.

Personal Residence and Other Real Estate

You can also use your home to fund a special-needs trust. Your home becomes a significant asset as you follow the Blueprints process and pay it off during your working years.

Homes work to build wealth when they are affordable. Your payment on a fixed-rate mortgage (including taxes and insurance) should not be more than 25 percent of your take-home pay. It is hard at best to enjoy your life and build wealth if your mortgage payment is too high.

Ideally, you should pay your home off before you retire, and you have the entire value of your home to fund the trust when you pass away. A trust can own the home, or your personal representative can sell it and transfer the proceeds to the trust.

Houses build wealth over time with money you have to spend somewhere anyway. Instead of paying rent toward someone else's wealth, you pay your mortgage and gain value each month. This asset can be used to fund a trust instead of being wasted on rent payments made over your lifetime.

Your family member with special needs will have to live someplace in the future. Many families want that place to be the family home. Some nonprofit organizations will make this possible and deliver services to your family member in her own home. Review your goals to see if you prefer to have your family member live independently after you are gone. If so, the family home may be the best place. This will help you know if the house should go to the trust and be used over the long term or if the home should be sold and the money received from the sale used for the trust and other beneficiaries.

People like a house to fund the trust because it is easy to understand as an asset. Houses are not stocks and bonds or complex financial instruments of any kind. It's a tangible asset—you can walk into it, feel it, and move around in it.

If you handle your home well, it can become a valuable asset. If not, it can become a burden.

Houses look great as investment assets because we can live in them and build wealth slowly. Unfortunately, it doesn't always work that way. For example, 2008 and 2009 saw a huge decline in the value of houses, and many families lost their homes to bankruptcy and foreclosure. These people had mortgages they could not afford and lost the chance to sell when the market collapsed. Houses take time to realize gains as an investment.

Homes also have some downsides to think about, and you will want to take steps to protect against these. For example, houses can be expensive to maintain. The roof will not last forever. Water leaks from showers, tubs, sinks, and ice makers could require new flooring or drywall. Property taxes are increased to support schools, libraries, and community needs. There are insurance costs. You will need yard tools—rakes, shovels, lawnmowers, snow or leaf blowers, and hoses. These add up quickly as you start a home or need replacement tools.

Renters can call the owner to get a new oven or furnace if it breaks; homeowners need to buy these replacements.

Houses do not always sell when needed. The trust may need cash from the house right away, but it may take time to sell the house. A person cannot wake up at 8 a.m. and decide to sell the house, then have cash in hand at the end of the day. The process of selling a house takes at least a month and can take longer depending on market conditions.

Selling a house can be expensive in and of itself. Real-estate agents charge a commission of about 6 percent on the sale of a house. Closing costs can add up to $5,000 or more. You may have to improve your house a bit to sell it at a fair market price by repainting rooms, redoing floors, and upgrading fixtures and appliances. You need to count on 10 to 15 percent of the expected selling price go to commissions, closing costs, taxes, and improvements just to get your house sold.

The current market value of your house may be very different than what you expect or what you paid for it. Neighborhoods change. If your house is losing value each year, you could end up with a home worth less than what you paid for it. The overall economy plays a role in the value of your home at any given time, and some regions change for the better while others either don't change or lose value. There can be a big difference in price based on zip codes and areas within zip codes. The reality is that your house could be worth much less than you think if you have not kept up on sale prices where you live.

Sometimes the worst thing you can do is leave your home to the trust and require that the home be owned by the trust forever. Give the trustee the flexibility to sell the home if the neighborhood changes, the trust needs to have different assets, or your family member can no longer live in the house.

The trustee needs to determine whether the house should be sold or kept. If the home is kept, the trust will be required to maintain the home and pay for upkeep, taxes, and insurance. This is money that can no longer be used to support your son or daughter. If you think the home may be kept, make sure to leave enough money in the trust for the expenses you need for your family member and then add all the expenses you expect will be needed to improve and maintain the home over time. This will increase the amount of funding you need for the trust overall, as the house cannot be used to pay for expenses unless it is sold.

Term Life Insurance

Term life insurance is an inexpensive way to protect your family. For tens or hundreds of dollars a month, you buy coverage of hundreds of thousands or millions of dollars.

You need to have term life insurance in place as you build wealth. Insurance is a great tool if it is ever needed on the road to family financial security. A person cannot be replaced. The love, affection, enthusiasm, activities, and role the person plays in the family can never be restored once someone passes away.

Life insurance is used to replace the income from a working person as a family creates wealth. For the most part, you use life insurance to replace the after-tax income that was used to pay for expenses, lost contributions to retirement accounts, and shortfalls in trust funding during working years.

Don't forget life insurance for stay-at-home spouses. The working spouse will need to hire someone for a period of time to handle the many activities and contributions that were made by the stay-at-home spouse.

When someone who has life insurance dies, the beneficiary is paid a lump sum. This money—whether $250,000 or $2,500,000—comes to the family without any income tax due. The insurance money counts toward a person's estate, and there may be estate taxes owed.

You are now required to designate a beneficiary when you take out a life insurance policy. The beneficiary can be the estate, a person, a trust, a business, or a nonprofit organization. Your choice depends on your financial situation today and where you wish to direct your money. Families starting the Blueprints process must get out of debt, build emergency funds, and learn to invest for retirement and future special-needs expenses. You will most likely have the insurance go to your partner or spouse first and to the special-needs trust and other children's trusts second.

Families who have built a strong foundation and see their vision coming to life may designate more of the life insurance benefit to the special-needs trust, since they have taken care of retirement and other family needs or are far enough along the way.

The beneficiary can be changed at any time as long as you own the policy and do not have an irrevocable beneficiary designation (which most of us should not). Your financial life will change and improve as you follow the Building Blocks, and you can adjust your life insurance to keep pace with those changes.

Proceeds from a death benefit come to your family and trust without them having to pay income taxes. The trustee does not have to think about the transaction costs needed for homes. The trustee does not have to reserve money for taxes, as is required with traditional IRAs. The trustee can use the money immediately to benefit for your family member with special needs.

Insurance companies fall under state regulators who review their financials for your protection. This system has worked well for the past and looks to be in good shape today. You want to find a top-rated life insurance company. Your insurance company is making a twenty-year commitment to you. You will pay premiums each month or yearly for a long time, and you need to know the company will be there to pay your family if needed.

It is simple to send money to the trust from a term life insurance policy. You fill out a beneficiary designation using language provided by your estate attorney. That's it. It's simple, easy, and quick. If the policy's death benefit gets paid, your personal representative and trustee work together to set up a trust account, and the life insurance company sends a check to the account.

There are almost no downsides to having term life insurance in place. You do have to be able to afford the premium and pay that premium every year until you have created enough assets that you do not need the insurance anymore.

Remember, the beneficiary designation is crucial when you have insurance. Do not designate your family member with special needs as the beneficiary. Designate the special-needs trust. If not handled the right way, this simple mistake can cause your family member with special needs to lose valuable benefits.

Potential Cash-Value Policies

There are other types of life-insurance policies in which part of the premium goes to an investment or cash-value account. The industry typically calls these "permanent life insurance" policies, and they go by the names of "whole life," "universal life," "indexed life," or "variable life." I call them potential cash-value policies. Like any life-insurance policy, you designate the beneficiaries; if the policy is in force at the time of your death, any death benefit goes to these beneficiaries. You would identify the trust as a beneficiary in this case.

These policies are sold with the idea that the death benefit is always in place, no matter what happens in the rest of your financial life. In my experience, I have seen too many policies where the owner would have been far better off investing in a conservative mix of stocks and bonds than putting money toward the investments in the insurance policies. See my book *Protect Your Family* for more on this. In fact, most policies I have seen have less money in the cash value than the owner could have had by just keeping the money in a bank account.

These types of policies can play a role in your financial life but only after every other Building Block has been in place for years. The biggest risk with these policies is that if you stop paying your premium because of an emergency or the need to fund retirement, you lose all the premium payments you have made as well as the death benefit.

Annuities

Annuities are investment contracts between you and an insurance company. The initial intention of annuities was to transfer risk of future income—you gave an insurance company a lump sum of money, and the company gave you money back for the rest of your life as income.

Today there are the traditional annuities and more—fixed annuities, indexed annuities, and variable annuities. These all seek to give you some guaranteed income or growth return until you need the money as an income stream. Most of the time, these annuities will not help you build real wealth, as the internal returns and access to cash limit your ability to earn growth and income.

Annuities are about the last asset you want to use to fund a special-needs trust. They have the same tax problems as traditional retirement accounts, since the growth of funds in the annuity coming into the trust is taxed at income-tax rates. Annuity contract rules can also lead to penalties if you need to access the account before a certain age. Also, there are often high commission charges built in that you pay as a cost in the annuity or if you access the money during a certain time period.

Other Types of Assets

There are several other types of assets shown in Building Block 3. Some people accumulate wealth in family businesses, rental real estate, art and other collectibles, and other private companies or partnerships. These complex assets could be great for the trust.

In these cases, you have to know first if your trustee has the ability, knowledge, and experience to handle these types of assets. You do not want to leave your fast-food franchise to the trust and have them run by a trustee who has never operated a business. You do not want a trustee to handle apartment-building management and mainte-nance if that trustee lives in a different state or country and has no experience hiring a property manager.

Each of these assets can be left to the trust, but make sure you understand how the assets will be able to be used to support your family member with special needs. A small apartment building that has a property manager may generate income to be used for special-needs expenses, where a piece of art must be sold to do the same. Your collection of antique motorcycle parts (that your wife cannot wait to give away) may not do any good if owned by the trust if they cannot be sold easily, but you may want to the trust to own it if your daughter loves the memories you made with her over time.

Discuss these assets with your financial team to determine whether or not they should be left to the special needs trust.

THE BEST LIFE POSSIBLE

A funded special-needs trust gives your family member the chance to live a life full of excitement, joy, and dignity. The assets in a trust help pay for those parts of life we all crave—entertainment, social life, travel, education, and anything else that makes life fulfilling. Without money in a trust, we leave our family members little more than a bare existence. With it, we leave a legacy to be felt and appreciated every day.

This is the fulfillment of the Blueprints process. You make decisions every day about how to live, how to spend or save money, and how to put your dreams and goals into action. The Building Blocks are designed to help you identify those goals and take the right action steps to make them happen. The process works best when we take care of ourselves and leave a legacy for our family member who needs support from us today and in the future.

Finishing Touches, Improvements, and Additions

From the moment you started Building Block 1, you made a commitment to improve your financial life and build the most enjoyable, fulfilling, and desirable life for yourself and your family member with special needs.

Most families do not live life with intention. They get pushed and pulled, blaming fate, bad luck, and poor habits as they keep getting derailed. Families who take Blueprints to heart put a stake in the ground and are ready to build the life and financial future they want. They take charge as they imagine wonderful times ahead and reduce their stress today as they get where they want to go.

You have a choice to make. You can put a stake in the ground to improve your life and protect your family member with special needs, or you can continue as you have been and compromise not only your own quality of life but the safety and protection of your family.

The choice is quite simple. Begin today. Go back to the beginning of this book, get out a piece of paper, and sketch out your hopes and dreams. Follow the Building Blocks in order to insure peace of mind and a high quality of life for each member of your family. It all starts with a simple sketch of your goals and dreams that will carry you through the good times and the bad as you build your dreams through financial security.

While the Blueprints process gets you to a place where you can live comfortably, it is not the end of the road.

Once you have finished all the Building Blocks, you will have the chance to put the finishing touches on your plan, your life's ambitions, and your wealth. When I speak to audiences, I meet people who have a special-needs trust in place but no plan to fund the trust, fund their retirement, or finance their other goals. They live on the foundation and think they are done.

Blueprints helps you build a financially and legally sound home. By the time you have finished all the Building Blocks, the key parts will be in place, and you can begin to add any finishing touches you need or want. You should have enough savings toward retirement, education, and the trust. The additional income you do not put toward daily life and future needs can be used to improve your life today, it can be used to make sure there are no leaks or gaps in your future plans, or it can be used to give back to your community.

Take the trip you have always wanted to take. Donate to the non-profits caring for your son or daughter. Create experiences that make lifelong memories for your family. Because you know you are taking care of your future needs by saving and investing wisely, you can do these things without stress, worry, or fear.

PRIVATE PLANES FOR A CLIENT

One of our clients had more money coming into his special-needs trust than he would ever spend. Part of his trust included royalty income from oil wells. His basic needs were met by SSI and Medicaid, and the money started to accumulate in the trust. This client had medical issues and could not be expected to live a long time.

His trustee decided to give him several gifts of a lifetime. The first was to get him to a world-class medical facility in another state. The person with special needs could then spend the time at the clinic getting all of his medical issues reviewed at once by a team that was focused on him. The Mayo and Cleveland Clinics are each famous for the improved outcomes of their work as a result of the deep, personal medical reviews coordinated by teams of people in different areas of expertise.

This client had a problem, however. He could not travel that far by car, nor could he fly in a commercial airplane as a result of his reaction to too many people in a confined space. The answer: the trustee hired a private plane. The trust paid the expenses to get the client to the medical clinic, then paid for his care once he was there. His life improved as a result, and he had his first real trip outside the state where he lived.

Next on the list for the client? The trustee decided to hire another plane, and he took the client on a vacation to Las Vegas. The client had never seen such a place, and it was a wonderful experience he could not have had without the special-needs trust.

This is a wonderful example of improvements and additions to a person's life that could not have been made without the right planning and use of a special-needs trust. Make a difference for your loved one with special needs today by using the Building Blocks to help you get out of debt, save for emergencies, and plan for retirement. When you take advantage of what the Blueprints program has to offer, you not only ensure quality of life for your family member with special needs but also create a world where you have the freedom and power to make your dreams come true. What are you waiting for?

WORKSHEETS

FIND TIME TO DREAM

Day of the week

Time of day

Location

Your DreamList

Write down anything and everything you want in life for yourself, your children, your community, and whatever else crosses your mind. Get it all out and written down.

_____   _____   _____

_____   _____   _____

_____   _____   _____

_____   _____   _____

_____   _____   _____

_____   _____   _____

_____   _____   _____

_____   _____   _____

_____   _____   _____

_____   _____   _____

_____   _____   _____

CLARIFY YOUR VALUES

A compass helps people orient themselves when lost. Knowing and understanding your values will help you when making complex decisions related to your planning. Write down several of the values you use to make decisions and the values you see for your family member with special needs.

Your Values:

_____

_____

_____

Values of Your Special-Needs Family Member:

_____

_____

_____

Examples:

Spiritual Life	Education	Family
Independent Living	Safety	Happiness
Order	Financial Wealth	Personal Exploration
Creativity	Arts	Neighbors
Community	Social Network	Integrity
Opportunity	Excellence	Success
Physical Health	Love	Employment Opportunities

Your Personal Strengths

Identify the positive personal characteristics that help you now and will help you in the future.

_____

_____

_____

_____

_____

Identify the positive personal characteristics that currently help you and that you will practice over the next three months.

_____

_____

_____

_____

_____

219

APPRECIATE TODAY

Write down what you appreciate in your life.

_____

_____

_____

_____

_____

Write down ways you appreciate your family member with special needs.

_____

_____

_____

_____

_____

MAP MY DREAMS

Family

_____

_____

_____

Special Needs

_____

_____

_____

Finances

_____

_____

_____

Recharge/Play/Spirituality

_____

_____

_____

Career

_____

_____

_____

Rewards

_____

_____

_____

BLUEPRINTS

Eliminate debt _____

Build emergency funds _____

Start retirement savings _____

Meet with an attorney _____

Plan to fund a trust _____

Top Ten

1.	6.
2.	7.
3.	8.
4.	9.
5.	10.

CELEBRATIONS AND REWARDS

Write down several different ways you can celebrate and reward yourself for the steps you have taken. These rewards should be of reasonable cost compared to the goal you have achieved. Some rewards do not need to have any cost, like taking a hike or carving out personal time for a hobby.

_____   _____   _____

_____   _____   _____

_____   _____   _____

Financial Checklist

You may have some or all of the following. Please provide account statements or other documents wherever possible.

- ❏ Bank account or credit union account statements
- ❏ Investment account statements
- ❏ Individual retirement accounts and employer retirement account statements, including 401(k) and 403(b) accounts
- ❏ Pension estimates and values
- ❏ Annuity statements
- ❏ Life insurance policy information (coverage summary pages and/or recent illustration)
- ❏ Real estate current values (include estimated purchase dates)
- ❏ Mortgage information—include current balance, interest rate, payment amount, number of years, and start date
- ❏ Credit card statements
- ❏ Student loan statements
- ❏ Homeowner's insurance and car insurance policy declaration pages
- ❏ List of significant personal property, such as automobiles, boats, jewelry
- ❏ Disability insurance policy page and last invoice
- ❏ Long-term care insurance policy page and last invoice
- ❏ Buy/sell agreements
- ❏ Business valuations
- ❏ Stock option plan information
- ❏ Deferred compensation contracts
- ❏ Social Security annual statement
- ❏ Collectibles information—such as coins, art, and antiques, and estimated values
- ❏ Beneficiary designations
- ❏ Other

ASSETS

Assets	Value	Financial Institution	Owner
Taxable Accounts			
Savings			
Checking			
Investment			
Retirement Accounts			
IRA			
Roth IRA			
401(k)			
403(b)			
Other Retirement			
Real Estate			
Primary Home			
Second Home			
Rental Property			
Education Accounts			
529 Plan			
Education IRA			
UGMA/UTMA			
Other Accounts			
ABLE Act			
Trust			
Annuity			
Business Interests			
Loans to others			
Vehicles			
Car 1			
Car 2			
Other			

DEBTS

Debts	Amount	Lender	Interest Rate	Minimum Payment	Start Date	Length of Loan
Mortgage/Home						
First						
Second						
HELOC						
Credit Cards						
Card 1						
Card 2						
Card 3						
Student Loans						
Loan 1						
Loan 2						
Vehicle Loans						
Loan 1						
Loan 2						
Other Debt						
Personal Loan						
Other 1						
Other 2						
Private Stock						
Loans to others						
Total						

Income

Income Sources	Income Source	Monthly Income	Annual Income	Date Paid
Employment				
My Income				
Spouse/Partner				
Second Job				
Pension				
Social Security				
Passive Income				
Rental Real Estate				
Business Income				
Investments				
Other Retirement				
Other				
Bonus				
Partner Distributions				
Royalties				
Trust Income				
Total				

KEY PEOPLE

Beneficiary Designation—Primary

People and Organizations   Percentage

_____   _____

_____   _____

_____   _____

_____   _____

_____   _____

_____   _____

_____   _____

Beneficiary Designation—Contingent

People and Organizations   Percentage

_____   _____

_____   _____

_____   _____

_____   _____

_____   _____

_____   _____

_____   _____

Personal Representative

_____

_____

_____

Trustee

People and Organizations

_____

_____

_____

_____

_____

Guardian

People and Organizations

_____

_____

_____

_____

_____

Choosing an Attorney

Names of three attorneys to interview:

1. _____

2. _____

3. _____

Questions to ask:

1. What is your experience working with families like mine?
2. How many third-party trusts do you write in a typical year?
3. How many first-party funded trusts do you write in a typical year?
4. Tell me about your continuing education in this area?
5. How do you charge? Flat fee or hourly?
6. In what states are you licensed to practice?
7. How long have you been an estate-planning attorney?
8. Can you provide references of recent clients?

Communicate Your Plans

List the people you need to speak with to discuss the changes you have made to your estate plan:

1. _____
2. _____
3. _____
4. _____
5. _____
6. _____
7. _____
8. _____

Take a few minutes to rehearse. I recommend using the following language:

"Mom and Dad [or insert name], we have taken steps to change our wills to protect [name of family member with special needs]. He/she can receive government benefits as a result of the steps we have taken. My planner/attorney recommended we speak to all family members and friends about this. [Name of person with special needs] cannot have any money. We will not leave anything to him/her when we pass away. We are talking to you to make sure you know how we are protecting those benefits. We do not know if you plan to include [name of person] in your will or as a beneficiary of any accounts. If you do, please let us know so we can give you the right information to protect [name of person]. Thank you for taking the time to listen.

FAMILY INCOME

Family Income	Income Source	Monthly Income	Annual Income	Pre-Tax (Y/N)
Employment				
My Income	_____	_____	_____	_____
Spouse Income	_____	_____	_____	_____
Second Job	_____	_____	_____	_____
Passive Income				
Rental Real Estate	_____	_____	_____	_____
Business Income	_____	_____	_____	_____
Investment Income	_____	_____	_____	_____
Other	_____	_____	_____	_____
Business/ Employment/Other				
Bonus	_____	_____	_____	_____
Partner Distributions	_____	_____	_____	_____
Trust Income	_____	_____	_____	_____
Total	_____	_____	_____	_____

FAMILY EXPENSE

Family Expenses	Monthly	Annually
Housing		
Rent/Mortgage Payment	_____	_____
Utilities	_____	_____
Maintenance/Repair	_____	_____
Landscaping	_____	_____
Insurance (Home)	_____	_____
Property Taxes	_____	_____
Other	_____	_____
Food/Dining		
Groceries	_____	_____
Dining	_____	_____
Automotive		
Car Payment	_____	_____
Insurance	_____	_____
Repair/Maintenance	_____	_____
Gas	_____	_____
Insurance Coverage		
Insurance	_____	_____
Medical Premium	_____	_____
Dental Premium	_____	_____
Vision Care Premium	_____	_____
Unreimbursed Medical	_____	_____
Life Insurance Premium	_____	_____
Care Assistance		
Live-in	_____	_____
Respite	_____	_____
Custodial	_____	_____
Other	_____	_____

Family Expenses	Monthly	Annually
Medical/Therapeutic		
Medical Visits		
Equipment		
Medicine		
Transportation		
Home Assistance		
Eyeglasses		
Employment		
Tuition		
Transportation		
Materials		
Personal Needs		
Beauty		
Phone		
Subscriptions		
TV/Cable/Internet		
Cleaning/Laundry		
Savings		
Emergency Funds		
Car		
Furniture		
TV		
Computer		
Appliances		
Other		
Special Equipment		
Wheelchair		
Hearing Aid/Batteries		
Other		

Family Expenses	Monthly	Annually
Other		
Beauty	_____	_____
Charitable Donations	_____	_____
Clothing	_____	_____
Dry Cleaning	_____	_____
Computer	_____	_____
Entertainment	_____	_____
Gifts	_____	_____
Insurances	_____	_____
Legal/Tax Prep	_____	_____
Loan Payments	_____	_____
Recreation	_____	_____
Religion	_____	_____
Sports/Fitness	_____	_____
Taxes	_____	_____
Vacation	_____	_____
Pet Care	_____	_____

Special Needs Expenses

Special Needs Expenses	Monthly	Annually
Housing		
Rent/Mortgage Payment	_____	_____
Utilities	_____	_____
Maintenance/Repair	_____	_____
Care Assistance		
Live-in	_____	_____
Respite	_____	_____
Custodial	_____	_____
Other	_____	_____
Medical/Therapeutic		
Medical Visits	_____	_____
Equipment	_____	_____
Medicine	_____	_____
Transportation	_____	_____
Home Assistance	_____	_____
Other		
	_____	_____
	_____	_____
	_____	_____
	_____	_____
	_____	_____
	_____	_____

Debts

Debts	Amount	Lender	Interest Rate	Minimum Payment	Start Date	Length of Loan
Mortgage/Home						
First						
Second						
HELOC						
Credit Cards						
Card 1						
Card 2						
Card 3						
Student Loans						
Loan 1						
Loan 2						
Vehicle Loans						
Loan 1						
Loan 2						
Other Debt						
Personal Loan						
Other 1						

CHOOSING A FINANCIAL PLANNER

Names of three advisors/planners to interview:

1. _____

2. _____

3. _____

Questions to ask:

1. What are your credentials and educational background?
2. How long have you been an advisor? How long has your firm been in business?
3. What makes you a good advisor?
4. What types of clients do you have?
5. How do you charge?
6. Do you use models or platforms or provide individualized portfolios?
7. Do you or your firm have any current or prior disciplinary issues?
8. Do you have a client specialty?
9. What services do you offer and most use with clients?
10. Do your clients get a written plan? Is there an additional cost?
11. How often will you communicate with me?
12. What is your experience working with families like mine?
13. Tell me about your approach to working with clients?
14. Ask yourself after interviewing an advisor the following: "Is this advisor sales-oriented or education-orientated?"

Funding a Trust

Decide the lump sum needed to fund a trust for your family member with special needs.

What will be required to support your family member with special needs? Families with young children with special needs will have to guess at the expenses. Those with older family members with special needs have a track record to use to calculate out of pocket expenses for additional medical and therapeutic treatments, entertainment and more. Use your budget worksheets to write down the costs. Multiply expected annual expenses by the number of years needed.

future special-needs
expenses per year   _____

times

number of years   _____

equals

amount needed for
special-needs expenses   _____

For example: $5,000 transportation expense plus $5,000 medical expense plus $5,000 other expense equals $15,000. This will be needed for 25 years. $15,000 times 25 equals $375,000.

GLOSSARY

This appendix provides a glossary of some of the terms you will come across when working with your attorney on the estate plan. It is provided to give you some basic understanding of the language of the estate plan so that you can be better prepared for your first meeting with your lawyer.

BASIC TERMS

The following are the key terms you need to be familiar with when you go to a lawyer. This short glossary will help you understand the key people to appoint and sections of an estate plan you will get from an attorney:

- Will
- Estate

- Personal representative
- Probate
- Trust
- Special-needs trust
- Financial powers of attorney
- Medical powers of attorney
- Living will
- HIPAA provisions
- Guardian
- Beneficiary
- Trustee
- Conservator
- Beneficiary designation
- Beneficiary deed

WILL

A will is a set of written instructions on how to dispose of your possessions and legal responsibilities after you die. This includes your debts, assets, and legal authority over children and any others for whom you have legal authority. Your will is the road map for the distribution of your estate.

Your will gives instructions on how to handle your assets. If you wish to leave your investments to your spouse, your house to a trust, and your coin collection to your nephew, you write this in a document called a will. Your will can direct all of your assets to go to a trust. It also tells your personal representative the name of the person you've chosen as guardian of your minor children when you pass away.

Wills can be simple or complex depending on your needs.

ESTATE

The word *estate* in legal planning stands for all that you own, all that you owe, and all for which you have legal responsibility. Your assets are items to which you have legal rights, interests, or entitlements. They include bank and investment accounts, real estate, business interests, loans you have to others, and more. Your liabilities include any money you owe to any other person or entity, like a mortgage, credit card debt, personal loans, divorce payments, and more. You have an estate whether you own or owe $1 or $1,000,000.

PERSONAL REPRESENTATIVE

Your personal representative (often called an executor) is the person you designate to represent you after you have died in handling the disposition of your assets and carrying out the terms of your will. This can be a family member, a friend, or a professional. The personal representative has the legal authority to pay your bills, sell property, and give money to those people, trusts, or institutions you've designated in your will.

PROBATE

Probate is the process of administering a person's estate. Debts have to be paid. Taxes must be filed. Remaining assets need to be sent to the right people or trusts. Guardianships must be established.

Through probate, notices are sent to anyone or any organization that may have an interest in the property of the deceased person. The personal representative files with a probate court and is granted authority over the estate to pay bills, transfer money, and help with children or guardians.

The probate court may require in-person hearings if there are people or companies fighting over the will (called "contesting a will"). The probate process works through the payment of monies, distribution of assets, and making of decisions about who receives what.

TRUST

Trusts are legal tools used to hold property. *Trust* used to be a term used when one person held property (asset) interests for the benefit of another, regardless of whether there was a document spelling it out. You wanted that person to be a "trusted" person. Now trusts are legal creations used to hold present or future interests of property. I can have my will create a trust when I die to hold money for my child with special needs or for my typical children.

Trusts can be complicated, as they are tools that can be used for many different purposes. One trust may hold money to be given to a charity. Another may be designed to hold property to protect against lawsuits. Another may be used to gift money to family members over time.

Blueprints uses trusts for two purposes. The primary purpose is the special-needs trust. You may also have a trust if you have other children. Many families do not want to leave money to young adults or minor children. Their portion of your estate could go into a different kind of trust that can be accessed as they get older or become responsible adults.

Trusts are used for many other reasons. Some states, like California, have high probate costs, and trusts are used to avoid probate. Other trusts are used when there are divorce issues, inheritances, or just to help a parent more effectively manage assets.

Trusts can allow for the person who controls the money to be different from the person who benefits from the money in the trust—something very important to Blueprints planning for people with special needs.

SPECIAL-NEEDS TRUST

In 1993, Congress passed legislation that led to the creation of types of trusts called special-needs trusts. These trusts allow a person with a qualifying disability to benefit from money in the trust without having the money (or other assets) in the trust be considered a countable resource. Remember, a person with special needs who has more than $2,000 in certain assets (called countable resources) cannot receive Supplemental Security Income.

Almost every person with a family member with special needs will need a special-needs trust. These trusts are sometimes called "supplemental" or "disability" trusts. There are three different types of special-needs trusts: first-party funded trusts, third-party funded trusts, and pooled-income trusts. If you set up your estate so your money goes into a third-party funded special-needs trust, you will not need the others. Blueprints is designed to avoid first-party and pooled-income trusts.

FINANCIAL POWERS OF ATTORNEY

Your estate plan will include instructions that allow someone else to act on your behalf at certain times. These instructions are called *powers of attorney*. You will have financial and medical powers of attorney in your estate documents.

Financial powers of attorney are used when you reach a point where you cannot handle your day-to-day finances. This may happen as a result of a medical emergency, aging, or some other event. These need to be part of your estate plan. Usually financial powers of attorney have provisions that allow a designated person to act under a set of specific circumstances.

Powers of attorney may be limited to specific actions, like

requesting information or signing documents to buy a house, or they may be broad, allowing the person with power of attorney to handle every aspect of a person's financial life.

MEDICAL POWERS OF ATTORNEY

Medical powers of attorney give authority to someone else to make medical decisions for you. The medical powers of attorney allow the person you name to speak with doctors, nurses, hospitals, and other key people involved in your medical care. They're given the authority to direct care or make medical decisions for you. You can outline the types of decisions you allow this person to make.

LIVING WILL

Your living will goes along with your medical power of attorney. The living will spells out whether you wish to be kept alive by artificial means (life support), including for how long and under what conditions. The living will becomes important when you are not likely to recover on your own with current medical interventions, and it is used to turn off or withhold treatment in a way you get to decide. Your living will tells the medical community who has authority to make these decisions and gives a trusted family member or friend the power to let your wishes be carried out.

Some of us will choose to stay alive in the hope that a cure will be found for whatever has caused the condition. More often than not, people choose to come off life support if there does not seem to be a strong likelihood of recovery. A living will reduces stress for those around you, as they can follow your directions instead of having to make a difficult decision on their own.

HIPAA Provisions

The Health Insurance Portability and Accountability Act of 1996 (HIPAA) is a comprehensive law designed to make changes to insurance and medical practices in the United States. A key provision of that act increases the privacy of patient information. An unintended consequence of the law was that it has become difficult for family members to talk with care providers in times of crisis or to arrange for ongoing care. These days, most attorneys include a HIPAA form when you get a will, and other necessary legal documents. The form gives permission for hospitals, doctors, and others in the medical community to speak with people you designate to help you.

Guardian

Your estate plan needs to include the appointment of a guardian (or guardians) if you have minor children. Have you thought about who will care for your family if you pass away while they are home with you as minors? Designate this person or family in your estate plan. Make sure you ask those people first. Do this in your estate plan; if you don't, the court becomes involved in deciding who can best raise your family.

You may need to become the guardian for your family member with special needs when she turns eighteen. This is a separate step you take while you are alive. Many people with special needs do not have guardians; they live independently and make their housing, care, employment, and financial decisions alone. Others need more help from parents, who become their legal guardians.

BENEFICIARY

A beneficiary is a person (or organization or trust) named to receive money in an account, a life insurance policy, a will, a trust, a deed, or any other contract that designates where assets will go. The beneficiary is the person who gets the money, usually when someone else passes away. The beneficiary of a special-needs trust is your family member with a disability.

TRUSTEE

The trustee is a person or corporation who handles the finances and assets of a trust. You choose the trustee when you set up a trust. At times, you may even be the trustee of your own trust. At times, you will choose someone else to act as trustee. The trustee must act in the best interests of and for the benefit of the trust beneficiary.

Like it sounds, you will want to find someone you "trust" to handle the money. This person should have shown an ability to handle money. The trustee is responsible to the beneficiaries of the trust and must pay money out of the trust if so required, prepare and pay taxes for the trust if necessary, and oversee the management of trust assets. Trustees can and usually do hire outside professionals for legal, tax, and investing duties.

CONSERVATOR

A conservator is basically a trustee appointed by a court. The duties of the conservator and trustee are about the same—the person uses and manages assets in the trust or conservatorship for the benefit of the person named. The biggest difference is that a conservator must report to the court, usually once a year. The court decides how the money will be spent. A trustee often has more choice on when to spend money and assets in the trust as long as it is done in a way that is in the best interests of the beneficiary.

BENEFICIARY DESIGNATION

A beneficiary designation is made on a form that acts as a contract when you open certain types of accounts or insurances. This is usually seen when you open a retirement account, take out a life insurance policy, buy an annuity, create a trust, or set up some other type of account where you want or are required to say where the money will go at what time. Beneficiary designation forms are the most overlooked part of special-needs planning, and you must make sure these forms match the rest of your estate plan.

BENEFICIARY DEED

Your home and real estate often represent a significant part of your estate. In the past, families had two ways they could tell the personal representative or probate court what to do with their house and other real estate. One was to put everything into a trust and then spell out in the trust how to handle the home and other real estate. The other was to let the home and other real estate become part of the probate estate and let the personal representative handle them.

Now there is a third option—the beneficiary deed. The beneficiary deed is like the beneficiary designation. The big difference is that the deed is used for real property—real estate, commodities, and land. It works the same as the beneficiary designation form on a retirement account: you name the person, people, or trusts that will receive your property. This allows the property to avoid probate and can make it easier to transfer the property from your estate to your chosen beneficiaries.

APPRECIATIONS

This book would not be finished and available without the assistance, support, and encouragement of many people. They deserve my deep and authentic appreciation of how they have helped me over time.

My family is incredible: fun to be with, busy with their lives and as proud of their Dad as I am of them (which is a ton). Thank you Benjie, Sarah, and Annie. I love you all and I love watching you grow, develop, and turn into wonderful people. Kelly Smith's patience, care and love keep me moving forward and I appreciate you being with me. My parents, Myra and Charlie, are supportive and have given me the education and work ethic that shapes me daily.

This book has been taking shape for years and got the boost it needed to get finished by the team at Quantum Leap. Special thanks to Martha Bullen and Deb Englander, two experienced publishing professionals, for their reading of the book and the encouragement to move forward. Geoffrey Berwind's expertise in storytelling aided in the understanding of how this book could help more people. Rose George, Gail Snyder, Tamra Richardt, Mary Giuseffi, Judy Cohen, Brian Edmondson, and Steve Harrison provided advice, support, cheerleading, assistance, and guidance to keep me on track and enthusiastic about the process.

Jerry Dorris designed the cover and interior and his cover design catches my goal of having works that are approachable, useable and energizing. Laurie Budgar, a good friend and amazing editor, helped make sense of my first efforts and influenced the style and tone for the book. The team at Eschler Editing of Kathy B. Jenkins and Michele Preisendorf offered excellent editing services and fantastic advice with their comments and suggestions. They were able to be flexible with my schedule and I appreciate that extra effort. Deana Riddle took this book from digital files to the finished product you hold today with her knowledge of publishing platforms.

The people I work with at Cascade Investment Group give me the ability to continue to offer excellent advice and service to my clients while having the time to write, publish and speak with families with a special-needs member. Scott Rethi manages to keep me on track at Cascade, read my drafts and enable my speaking to groups. I appreciate and enjoy getting to work with Ken Beach, Dana Capozzella, Felicia Deal and Jan Weiland in our pursuit of excellence in service to our clients.

A few years ago, four of us started a new group that met weekly to encourage each other to pursue our dreams and offer advice and friendship. Thank you to Enclave group, Lisa Tessarowicz, Andrea Barker, and Kimberley Sherwood for pushing my efforts along to this point. I look forward to our meetings every time we get together.

My community in Colorado Springs is filled with caring,

compassionate and thoughtful leaders and professionals who serve individuals with developmental disabilities and their families. Ann Turner, Wil Romero, Donna Butzin, Jeannie Porter, Jeanne Solze, Steve Ogle, Lynn Perry, Spencer Gresham, David Ervin, Christina Butero, Gin Woolsey, Sheila Ferguson, Ann Koenigsman, Rabea Taylor, Patricia Yeager, Tom O'Neal, Julie Harmon, and John Urbanski have all been helpful in researching issues, making connections and providing opportunities for me to speak with families to sharpen the content of the book. There are many others and I am grateful for your help.

My daughter Sarah has had incredible opportunities in large part as a result of wonderful people who have gone the extra step to support her in school, health, community activities and in her social life. Thank you to the therapists, doctors, community members, friends, educators, and everyone who works with and supports our family and to everyone else involved with us.

About the Author

ROB WRUBEL, CFP° AIF° is the creator of *Blueprints* a financial planning process to help families with a special-needs member get out of debt, save for retirement, and protect and enhance potential government benefits for their family member with special needs. He is a Senior Vice President, Investments with Cascade Investment Group in Colorado Springs, CO.

Rob has three children. His middle child was born in 2003 and she has Down syndrome. A few months after her birth, Rob began to research how financial planning for a family with a special-needs member is different than planning for a typical family. He has focused his practice on working with families with special-needs members and the professionals and organizations that serve them.

He donates time through his direct support of several organizations. He currently serves as Vice-President of the Board of Directors

256   *Financial Freedom for* SPECIAL NEEDS FAMILIES

of the Pikes Peak Community Foundation and as Co-Chair of a capital campaign for The Arc Pikes Peak Region. He has served as President of the Cheyenne Village Board of Directors and CASA of the Pikes Peak Region. He has served on the Boards of Directors of the Ronald McDonald House Charities of Southern Colorado, the Colorado Fund for People with Disabilities and the Colorado Springs Down Syndrome Association.

Rob is a New Jersey native and graduate of Wesleyan University in Middletown, CT.

Find out more about Rob, his publications or for booking information to hire Rob to speak at an event at www.robwrubel.com.

Made in the USA
Las Vegas, NV
25 February 2022

44552122R00154